Frau Elizabeth Schwyzer
Festal Costume, Zurich, 1564.

By Tobias Stimmer

COSTUME AND CONDUCT

IN THE LAWS OF

BASEL, BERN, AND ZURICH

1370–1800

BY

JOHN MARTIN VINCENT

Professor Emeritus of History
The Johns Hopkins University

GREENWOOD PRESS, PUBLISHERS
NEW YORK

TO MY WIFE

AID AND COMPANION THROUGH
MANY YEARS

PREFACE

This small volume is a condensation of materials found in the printed laws of Switzerland and in the manuscript deposits in the archives of Basel, Bern and Zurich. It is a part of extensive studies in the sumptuary regulations of France, England and Germany and selected for publication because of the contemporary records of enforcement which these Swiss cities have preserved. Their laws are not singular, for they represent the spirit of the age of their enactment, but the recorded action of their judicial tribunals in the matter of costume and conduct are exceptionally extensive and illuminating.

The rules respecting Sabbath observance and profanity are not strictly sumptuary in character, but they exhibit the scriptural basis upon which the regulation of conduct was founded and are included here because they lay within the jurisdiction of the same courts which passed judgment on the dress of their constituents. Together they lead to deeper penetration into the social ideals of their day.

The author is under obligations to many books and persons for assistance in the accumulation of facts and the preparation of the narrative. The archivists of Basel, Bern and Zurich freely displayed their treasures to a grateful inquirer. Professor Kent Roberts Greenfield gave valuable suggestions toward the form of presentation and Dr. Emily W. Emmart with sure touch of her pen added many drawings to the illustrations of costume.

French and German pictures of dress have been included in this narrative for the reason that during a large part of the period France, the dictator of fashion, was faithfully imitated by Germany, and together they displayed the modes and fancies which the Swiss laws endeavored to restrict.

TABLE OF CONTENTS

LIST OF ILLUSTRATIONS

LIST OF ILLUSTRATIONS

COSTUME AND CONDUCT

IN THE LAWS OF

BASEL, BERN, AND ZURICH

1370–1800

I. INTRODUCTION

THE management of private conduct by means of police regulations and sumptuary laws began early among the ancients. The Roman Law contains regulations of this character and the Middle Ages as soon as codes of law became regularly established continued industriously in this line. It would be a mistake however to think that generations followed one another simply according to situation, because there is a principle behind this form of law which is clearly in evidence throughout a long period of time. That principle is the conception of the interest and duty which governments believed they had in all their subjects, not only in their political and legal behavior but also in their moral and spiritual welfare. Concern for these latter was particularly strong in the Middle Ages, as we shall frequently have occasion to observe, and religious and paternal interest is strikingly conspicuous throughout the three centuries which we are about to contemplate.

Ordinances of certain cities of Switzerland are here brought to view, not because of their singularity, but because they are typical of other regions of central Europe where local government was not under the control of national legislation. In France and England sumptuary laws were either the product of royal decree or of national statute, but in Germany where semi-independent states and cities were numbered by hundreds the regulation of personal conduct fell to local authorities. Nuremberg, Strassburg, Hamburg, Lübeck and many other cities of central Germany issued sumptuary ordinances similar in character and differing only in detail. So the absence of central government in Switzerland left to the great cities like Zurich, Basel, and others the duty of making and administering their own laws, both in political matters and minor police regulations.

The paternal conception of government appears plainly enough in the Swiss legislation, for the preambles of ordi-

1

nances and the interjected advice leave no doubt of the intentions of the city fathers. This characteristic is potent throughout the whole period from the fourteenth to the eighteenth century, and to understand why the principles lasted so long we have to stop for a moment to consider the political history of Switzerland.

For more than five hundred years the Swiss Confederation from its beginning down to 1848 was a group of small states, each jealous of its own sovereignty under a central union which was practically innocuous. This group of states, often threatened from the outside, held together sufficiently to protect its independence but each part managed its own affairs. The cities of Zurich, Bern, and Basel were the most important. Their governments carried out all the functions of peace and war. Inside of their city walls they conducted diplomacy, regulated legal procedure, governed outside provinces, regulated trades and gilds, and paved their streets with cobblestones. Their governments were essentially aristocratic. In Bern this was an actual fact, while in Basel and Zurich the gilds had in the course of time gained a place in the city council. In these latter cities the most representative body was the Council of Two Hundred who were called into action for the confirmation of certain kinds of legislation. (Figure 1.) In Bern the government was actually an aristocracy of family, though in Zurich and Basel, notwithstanding the partial extension of the electorate, the spirit of the government was essentially the same, a form which might have been called a "Business Aristocracy." Thus we have the paternal conception of government linked to an effectual rule of the upper classes. In the ordinances passed by these authorities a strong religious motive is abundantly evident when they attempt the regulation of personal conduct. In so many words they endeavor to enforce the ten commandments, proclaim against profanity, the neglect of the Sabbath, and the extravagances of luxury as displeasing in the sight of God. To them the wrath of God was clearly to be seen in earthquakes, the desolations of war, or the failure of crops, and to obtain relief the people must give heed to their ordinances. To make sure that ignorance of the law should not be an excuse for disobedience it was decreed that the regulations on conduct should be read from the pulpit once every year. Thus church and state were in active co-operation in the enforcement of these rules, yet it must be remembered that such ordinances were not the acts of ecclesiastical synods, but the decrees of secular governments, and formed only a very small portion of the business and enact-

Fig. 1. Basel. Members of Council in Festal Hats.
" Gugelhut."   Middle of 17th Century.

ments which claimed their attention. Clerical members were included in many of their administrative divisions and doubtless had much to say in the wording of the mandates which we are to consider, but these are essentially the product of the political and secular atmosphere of the time in which they occur.

In the cities of Basel, Bern, and Zurich previous to the Reformation the administration of sumptuary and moral laws was entrusted to an ecclesiastical court called the *Chor-Gericht*. This body also had jurisdiction in cases of adultery and marriage relations, since according to the sacramental conception of marriage such cases were subject to the discipline of the church. In the sixteenth century, owing to the Reformation and to certain secularizing tendencies, these functions in some places were separated. Marriage relations were left to the ecclesiastical tribunal, and a new court was erected for the administration of sumptuary laws. Chosen by the city council from among men of mature age and excellent reputation this body continued to function for a long time under a name equivalent to our " select men," and its history is continuous, although minor changes in organization took place from time to time. During the last third of the seventeenth century it became definitely known as the " Reformation-Chamber " (*Reformations-Kammer*, or *Reformations-Rath*), a word which at that time meant reformation of manners and morals rather than a reconstruction of theological doctrine. Under this title the court continued to function until the eve of the French Revolution, and the duties of the officials will appear as we proceed to consider the ordinances under which they operated.

Two important aspects give direction to any study of this matter. One lies in the contents of the ordinances themselves as they were promulgated from time to time. From the fourteenth to the end of the eighteenth century there is sufficient evidence in manuscript and in print to show the sequence and variation of these laws. There is no difficulty in tracing from decade to decade the attitude of city councils on the subject of personal conduct and its regulation.

A second aspect of the question is the execution of these prescriptions, and here the absence or loss of early records makes it difficult to ascertain completely either the intentions or the diligence of the administrators. By the mournful tone of their preambles and by the frequency of the reenactments it would appear that the observance left much to be desired. Not till late in the seventeenth century do the records become continuous, and even after that many gaps leave us in the dark as to the success or failure of such regulations.

Yet, notwithstanding the difficulties encountered in the subject, the rise and decline of sumptuary ordinances can be followed. In them will be found not only the legal conceptions of the lawmakers, but to the discriminating reader there will appear many sidelights on the social customs and personal habits of good and bad citizens at various periods and under various circumstances. From the records of the courts which punished infractions of these laws some conclusions may be drawn as to the value and effectiveness of sumptuary measures.

Although sumptuary legislation was a subject for local government, it will be well to consider a little further the general constitutional situation in which the cities were enveloped, for in that lies the explanation of their autonomy. In brief they had all grown up slowly from 1291 into a Swiss Confederation which after 1501 included thirteen cantons. This union was not based upon a single constitution but upon a complexity of treaties made between the separate states at various times and containing various conditions. The principal evidence of the union was a Diet comprised of delegates from each of these states which met from time to time and discussed questions of general interest. This Diet, however, had no power to enforce its own decrees, and consequently its acts were merely recommendations concerning which the cantons could do as they pleased. It passed several sumptuary regulations, but there was no federal authority which might put them in force. When the country was invaded by foreign powers there was something like unity of action, for they feared for their local preservation. War among themselves occurred from time to time, especially when issues were sharpened by religious animosity. Hence we are looking upon conditions where local government and even the most important affairs of state were left to the discretion of the cantonal authorities themselves. No regulations could be imposed upon any state against its own consent.

Prominent members of this confederation were Basel, Bern, and Zurich, each a city commanding adjacent territory of varied dimensions and holding its rural inhabitants in economic subjection. None of these towns contained more than ten thousand inhabitants, and, owing to the fear of war which might break out at any time, their narrow streets were surrounded by heavy walls and fortifications which must be maintained and guarded by the citizens themselves. Outside the walls the city authorities maintained a control over considerable territory, with a population which has long since

Fig. 2. Bern. Member of Council of Two Hundred. Early 18th Century.

been transformed into modern equality and the state has become one political unit.

During the period which we have under consideration city government was in the hands of a Small Council, which carried on the daily routine of business, and a Great Council, or Council of Two Hundred which was called together from time to time to sanction acts of prime importance. (Figure 2.) The chief figure in the picture is a Burgermaster, and under him are treasurers, tax collectors, and other necessary officials, either appointed or elected by one or more of the city councils. It was late in the fourteenth century that gilds became influential in city government, and thenceforward the heads or representatives of these trade organizations have a fixed place in the councils of the city, with powers which varied greatly in the three cities which we are examining.

This rough summary will serve to locate the responsibility for the sumptuary legislation, but we should miss the point in the situation if we overlooked the fact that in all these cases the governments were actually aristocratic, whatever may have been the title under which they acted. In Bern this was especially true, where the aristocracy had gained a predominance in the holding of important offices, while in Basel and Zurich, with certain limitations, the same phenomenon appears. In these latter cities the original aristocracy was slowly dying away, but the perpetuation of families in office and the self-renewal of many boards brought about a similar result. The common population found it burdensome to take part in legislation or serve in law courts, and thus the ruling of the city fell into the hands of the upper class. This had the advantage of gaining the services of those who were engaged in large business which was sometimes international in scope, or of men of the better educated class, yet this did not wholly mitigate the rigid ruling and selfish action of an aristocratic government. In spite of all this, however, we are obliged to admire the ability and versatility of government and the men concerned in it who were obliged to be prepared to undertake war, carry on intricate diplomatic negotiations, and at the same time oversee everything in a city, from the forms of church worship to the dress of its citizens and the price of a hair cut.

This admiration by no means assumes that there was no selfishness, bribery, or political corruption among these officials, for evidence of these evils is sufficiently recorded; but the wide variety of talent and information required for the administration of these small cities should not go without mention.

In each of these towns a commission was appointed to carry out sumptuary and minor police regulations. The bases of their powers were not simply police orders, but were ordinances passed by the highest legislative authority, and usually start with the phrase, " We, Burgermaster, Small and Great Council," (*Klein und Grosser Rath*), and thus had the sanction of serious city laws. The courts appointed for the execution of the ordinances have a somewhat various history as to form, but throughout the whole period they were manned by citizens of high official position or reputation.

Previous to the Reformation and in some instances long after, delinquencies of this kind were brought before the ecclesiastical court, which had jurisdiction over marital relations and other serious questions, called the *Chor-Gericht*, or Consistory, a situation quite in accord with the conception of clerical powers found in England and other places in that period. (Figure 3.)

After the Protestant Reformation these duties remained about the same as before, but the members were responsible to the council of the city. In Bern the *Chor-Gericht* retained jurisdiction over sumptuary matters till late in the seventeenth century, as may be seen from an ordinance of 1667. In 1672 and for many years afterwards the execution of such laws lay in the hands of a smaller court of seven members known as the *Reformations-Executores*. After 1696 there is a break in the Bernese records of this tribunal lasting nearly a century, and when they begin again in 1782 the name Reform Council (*Reformations-Rath*) continues to 1797, when the activities of this body came to a close.

In Basel a semi-secularization took place much earlier, so that when we reach the seventeenth century there is an ordinance of 1637, for example, which gives jurisdiction to a body of *Inspectores* consisting of seven members, three from the council, two from the clergy, and two from the community at large. Through the greater part of the eighteenth century this court in Basel was known as the *Reformations-Geordnete*. In Zurich this authority after the Reformation was made even more secular when the jurisdiction was taken from the *Chor-Gericht* and administered under the eye of the city council. For the city district itself this new body consisted of twelve members, eight from the Small Council, and four from the Great Council, as may be seen in the ordinance of 1650. Here it functioned under the name of Reformation-

Fig. 3. Bern.
Consistory or Chorgericht, after 1528.
Jurisdiction included Sumptuary Laws.

Chamber (*Reformations-Kammer*), a title which it retained to the close of the eighteenth century. As to this designation it is hardly necessary to repeat that the word " Reformation " in this connection does not refer to changes in theology, as it might have done at an earlier date, but indicates rather that the tribunal is concerned with the reformation of the manners and morals of the community.

All three of these courts heard cases on other subjects than dress, expenditure, or extravagance; for assault and battery, scandalous reports, and other minor police matters came within their purview. As to the persons who acted as judges, we are left in no doubt as to their dignity and importance. They were not mere aspirants for office or fees, but were selected from the high officials of the cities, in some cases it being prescribed in the law that they must be men of mature age and experience of life.

Mayor.   Court   Sheriff.   Collector.   Constable.   Messenger.
           Recorder.

Fig. 4.   Bern.   City Officials, 17th Century.   By Conrad Meyer.

Judged from the records, the *Reformations-Kammer* of Basel was the most regular and assiduous in attendance upon business. The ordinance of 1637, for example, required this body to meet at least once a week, and the minutes show that for more than a hundred years they sat regularly on a Wednesday or a Monday. In Zurich, except for a few items from the seventeenth century, the minutes cover only the eighteenth, while in Bern the record is still more fragmentary. In all three of these cities it is evident that diligence in holding meetings of this court declined seriously after 1750, both in regard to the number of sessions and in the regularity of dates.

In the treatment of the subjects followed in this study no attempt will be made to give a complete picture of the activities of the *Reformations-Kammer* or its counterpart in the three cities. From the matters coming before these courts, such topics have been selected which affected more or less intimately the life of the citizens, and from which side-lights are thrown upon social customs and social conditions. Profanity and Sabbath observance have been included on account of the intimate relations of church and state and because the regulations display the powers of government in respect to personal conduct and religious duty. (Figure 4.)

II. PROFANITY

 IN the great ordinances issued from time to time, either the first or the second subject is profanity. The gravity of the offense can here be measured through more than four centuries, and the Protestant Reformation led to no weakening of the laws, but rather sharpened the penalties. Whether it was regarded as a personal or as a social evil, it is evident that the ordinances were based upon the scriptural commandments which the authorities felt compelled to uphold, in order to enforce respect for a Creator whose ill will they wished to avoid. Similarity of religious belief made these ordinances very much alike, although there were differences in the penalties and variety in the times when changes are introduced. Severity of punishment was much greater in the sixteenth than it was in the eighteenth century, while difficulty in enforcing obedience is visible throughout their whole history.

In the records of Zurich an ordinance of 1344 fixed the fine for profanity at sixpence, and if the fine was not paid the guilty person might expect banishment from the city. If he came back into the city before the expiration of the time, he might spend eight days in jail. During this early period a list of prohibited oaths was prescribed. God's wounds, God's sweat, God's head, God's lungs, God's beard, God's blood, and various other features of His anatomy were forbidden. From time to time changes were made in this list, because expressions went out of use and others were commonly adopted.

In the early days of the Protestant Reformation profanity even brought on capital punishment. In 1520 three men were executed for this crime, one of whom had destroyed with his sword an image of Christ on the cross, and the other had spoken or written forbidden curse words. In 1529 Hans Dahinden was condemned to death by the sword because he had sworn by " God's suffering," " God's power," " God's cross," and various other profane expressions, and had said, furthermore, "God knows nothing about me, but that is all the same to me, for if God does nothing for me the devil is

Fig. 5. Zurich. High Court of Law about 1580, by Daniel Lindtmayer.

For serious crimes and controversies.

my fast friend." In 1530 Hans Meier escaped death on petition of his friends, and the penalty was commuted to a heavy fine with costs. Furthermore he must on the coming Sunday

go to the church of his parish, stand in the pulpit, and call
on the people to pray for his forgiveness. He must not carry
any kind of a weapon, must forego all drinking or treating,
and be in his house by bedtime.

That same year Oswald Sutor laughed at the people who
warned him against profanity and said the devil would thank
them if they did not report him. He fled the country, but his
case was brought up, and he was likewise ordered to appear
in the pulpit. In 1532 Felix Meier was fined 100 gulden for
cursing and filthy words. Yet it seems that technicalities
could intervene in favor of the accused. In 1533 a letter
from the City Council to the governor of the district of
Knonau inquires as to a man held in Zurich for profanity
whether he had actually used swear words. Did he say
"God's wounds," or was it "Gat's wounds?" Judgment
would be suspended till they heard from the governor. One
may note in passing the antiquity of the word "gad" as a
supposedly innocent substitute in our less polite contemporary
vocabulary.

In all three cities the ordinances for the punishment of
profanity bear a close resemblance. Sometimes a fine is introduced, but for ordinary everyday swearing a public apology
and acts of penance form the requirements of the law. In
Zurich in 1765 there was a special ordinance on this offense.
From the language of this act, which seems particularly
sharp, the possibilities of punishment were prison, chastise-
ment, being haled before the ecclesiastical consistory, made
to sit under the pulpit, or exclusion from the sacrament, if
any of these things are necessary according to God's laws
and ordinances. As late as 1785 the ordinance gave warning
that the earlier laws would be enforced and the previous
penalties were repeated. Yet if we look into the minutes of
the Reformation-Chamber, which cover nearly all of the
eighteenth century, we find that in 1710 there were during
that whole year two cases of profanity brought before the
court, one of which paid a fine of five pounds. In 1714 and
1718 two more cases are on record, and during the remain-

ing seventy-nine years of the life of the tribunal not a single person was tried for this offense.

The record of the similar court in Basel covers the period of 122 years from 1674 to 1796, and the prosecutions for profanity are scarce. In 1681 there were ten cases among an annual total of 289 for all offenses, and in 1682 five out of 156. During fifteen later years selected because of the activity of the Reformation-Chamber and covering more than a century, there appear only five cases for cursing, and these were scattered over three different years.

III. SABBATH OBSERVANCE

THE observance of the Sabbath came down from the Middle Ages, not only because it was a habit accumulated through the centuries, dating back to early Christianity and the Hebrews, but because it was a scriptural command imposed upon the consciences of mankind which both religious and secular authorities felt bound to enforce. Sunday laws existed everywhere in Europe, and the Protestant Reformation quickened the consciences of all parties in that controversy, so that the question was not so much a matter of theological doctrines as it was an interpretation of this divine command and of the extent to which infractions should be punished.

On this subject the Swiss cities agreed with the rest of the world, and the secular authorities were called upon to assist in the enforcement of the ordinances. For the three centuries which we are considering their laws are very much alike. To the last moment of the eighteenth century they were issuing regulations for the use of that day of the week, and the only reason for the study of this form of the law is that we may gain another view of the powers of government, and inquire whether such rules were actually enforced. Local situations and peculiarities brought out rules of conduct which deserve consideration.

For particularity of detail an ordinance of Basel of 1637 is of much interest. Here the rules for Sunday observance are found in the so-called "Great Ordinance," and occupy twelve pages at the very beginning of that document. The mandate begins with an admonition that attendance upon public worship is necessary, and all people should be present and give solemn attention. Parents should see to it that their children and servants attend these ceremonies. On Sundays and feast-days there should be no work except that allowed by the word of God. All labor in field or house which prevents attendance on public worship is totally forbidden. Stores, shops, bakeries must be closed except for some unusual reason. Travelers passing through the city may need some slight repairs to their vehicles, but these must not be made during morning or evening services, and no new work like the making of cart-wheels, barrels, and such like may be undertaken on Sunday. As soon as the last bell rings for morning or evening meetings the city gates are to be closed, and are not to be opened until service is over. No drinking, gaming, feasting, or the like may take place during the day in gild houses, taverns, liquor shops, tennis courts, barber shops, or private houses. Taverns should serve their meals on time and the guests be urged to attend the religious services. Wine houses must be closed after three o'clock in the afternoon, and no one shall be served during the evening service hour. Nothing may be sold in the grain and fish markets during morning service. As soon as the second bell rings native merchants shall go home and attend worship, market people from the country shall cover up their wares and shall not go running about the market place, but sit still till the service is over, when they may resume their selling. Butcher shops must be closed, and the slaughtering of beasts is forbidden during church hours. Mills of all kinds must stop their wheels, and the carrying of grain to these is forbidden.

On Sundays no one may walk up and down on St. Peter's Platz, go into secret places to play cards, or commit other wanton acts. Certain exceptions are made for the Honorable Rifle Shooters and the Crossbow Society. The first may follow its old custom and have rifle practice on Sunday, but without noise or confusion, nor may they admit to their quarters persons who come there just for the eating and drinking, and they must urge everyone to attend evening service. The crossbow shooters are directed to attend evening service diligently, after which they may proceed with their target practice.

Going out of the city to collect debts with consequent neglect of church services is subject to fine. Likewise, a penalty will be imposed upon anyone who goes out on Saturday in order to collect debts on Sunday. Men or women, young or old, native or foreign, who walk about the streets during the morning or evening service, whether or not they have been to the early morning worship, or if found walking outside the city gates or idly sitting and gossiping before their houses, will be fined. If any one is hindered by illness so that he cannot attend worship in person, he must remain in his house, have his own religious service, and not be seen upon the street except for satisfactory reasons. House-holders are admonished to arrange their affairs so that their servants, whatever may be their religion, may attend worship within the city and not be obliged to go outside except on certain high feast-days.

Tuesday evenings there was also a service which all people must attend, if physically able, and shops must be closed. Promenading on the streets or the Rhine bridge must cease, and no driving of carts or wagons past the church, nor wash-ing of barrels at the fountains will be allowed. These rules also cover the monthly day of prayer.

The council records with sorrow that their subjects in the rural districts are not paying attention to the Sunday regula-tions. Many put off till Sunday things which they can do just as well during the week. On that day weddings, christen-ings, making of contracts, and many such things, along with eating, drinking, gaming, dancing, and other excesses of a shameless character take place. In view of " these evil times " the country people are admonished to attend worship and postpone to other days of the week any work which the Lord permits. Anyone who is so bold as to act contrary to this mandate shall be turned over to the local magistrates for trial or eventually be brought before the council. Country governors were especially warned to give attention to this matter. Execution of the ordinance was at this time in the hands of " Inspectores " consisting of three from the Small Council, two from the clergy, and two from the community at large.

Ordinances regulating the use of Sunday were issued in all three of these cities from time to time till the close of the eighteenth century, and while they differ somewhat accord-ing to locality, and the fines for non-observance differ in

amount, yet the spirit of the laws is everywhere the same.
In Basel the ordinance of 1715 is practically the same as that
of 1637, issued seventy-eight years earlier, both as to subjects
regulated and space devoted to their description. The ordinance of 1727 occupied only two pages, in place of the
twelve devoted to Sunday observance in 1637, and throughout the remainder of our period the rules are stated with
brevity. The fines were sometimes increased, but we are not
always sure whether this was due to greater severity or to
changes in the value of the currency.

In all these laws costume for the church is regulated, both
for men and women, and in all cases it is the most dignified
dress the time produced. In earlier days men must appear in
ruffs and black mantles, and whatever may have been the
fashion, the clothing should be dark. Women must also
wear only dark clothing in church, and upon their heads the
white headdress similar to a nun's covering and known as
the "*Tuechli.*" Expensive jewelry and even gold-mounted
prayerbooks were forbidden, such rules being intended to
give sobriety to the act of worship. Exceptions in the matter
of dress were sometimes made in favor of the very poor, but
throughout the whole period the attempt was made to reduce
by law the amount of display allowed to men and women
while attending public worship. This matter receives further
consideration later, in connection with the general subject of
dress.

Basel and Zurich each had a problem which involved them
in difficulties of administration, in that both cities had ordinances preventing people from going outside the walls
during the hours of religious services. These rules were not
so much a separate subject of law as an attempt to strengthen
the enforcement of Sabbath observance, especially attendance
at church. At the last stroke of the bell for morning service
the city gates were closed, and no one could go out until
worship was over except on a pass, or token, issued by a
member of the Chamber of Reformation. The gates were
again closed during the afternoon service.

The effectiveness cannot well be determined before the

later part of the seventeenth and during the eighteenth century, when the records of the Reformation Court become available. Exit from the gates was, to be sure, in the hands of members of the tribunal, but the number of tokens at their disposal was quite limited; and as a consequence we find that during the early years of the period the prosecutions for being outside were quite numerous. During the last fifty years the cases gradually fade out, but we can hardly assume that this was due to increase of respect for the law. What happened can be studied to better advantage later on in connection with the enforcement of other regulations.

Shooting with guns or bows and arrows had deep roots in Swiss life, and consequently these sports were permitted on Sunday between the hours of service, but these shooting stands must not be open for persons who used them merely for eating and drinking.

Other minor police regulations need not be listed here, for we have evidence enough to show that Sunday ordinances were based chiefly on religious commands, for the carrying out of which the secular government was under deep obligations. At one point the use of animals was forbidden, since horses and beasts of draft deserved a day of rest, while for mankind, a less controllable animal, there was provided by law a period of relaxation.

IV. CHRISTENINGS

AS the governments of Basel, Bern, and Zurich supported the same religion, whether before or after the Reformation, the regulations of baptism are naturally similar. Sponsors were limited to three, all of whom must have taken the communion, for no young person could act in that capacity before Confirmation, while the child must be brought to the font from three to fourteen days after birth, according to local practice.

The sumptuary aspect of such occasions appears in the limitation of gifts and festivities, and occasionally an attempt to regulate the clothing to be worn. The gift allowable from each sponsor varied from three shillings in 1336 to one or two ducats in the eighteenth century, but changes in purchase power must be taken into consideration. The essential point lies in the moderate value prescribed and the attempt to govern expenditure by law.

The ordinance of Basel in 1637 covers these points with particularity. Following a complaint that for some time christenings have displayed too much superfluous expense and that other pernicious misuses have crept in and daily become worse, the city council proceeds to renew the ordinance of 1612, and commands obedience under penalty of one mark in silver. The three sponsors may not give more than one gulden each, and the money must be enclosed in a packet and handed to the pastor, who shall examine it after the ceremony to see that only the lawful amount is presented. If the limit has been exceeded he will report to the Reformation Court, and if he fails in this duty he will be held responsible by the proper authorities.

This gift must not be supplemented by the so-called Sponsor-Coat, or fur robe, for the child, nor by any other extravagant gift. Furthermore, christening suppers, or the giving of dinners to guests after the ceremony, offering sweet wine and confectionery are all entirely forbidden (*gar und*

Fig. 6. Christening. 1751. By David Herrliberger.

gäntzlich abgestellt). Most earnestly reminding all women in child-bed to be careful they are ordered to avoid at christenings the abominable headdresses with vexatious laces towering above them, also sleeves made of satin, silk, or other costly material, or any such sumptuously adorned with gold or silver cords. Likewise, all excess and costliness in general must stopped, and in particular in baptismal outfits (*Tauf-zeug*), as well as the ornamentation of hangings, coverings, and bed clothing, while parents must strive to show true thankfulness for evident help and grace, and all honesty in avoiding the penalties of the law. (Figure 6.)

Restrictions in the number of visitors to the bedside were evidently in the interest of the sick mother, and begin early in the ordinances. For example, in Zurich in 1422 she may not give a "Cookie-Treat" to any but sponsors and near relatives; other callers must be content with a glass of wine. By 1488 the authorities found even this too much and abolished the cookie day and said there might be no refreshment for the women assistants beyond a glass of wine. Exception was made for ladies of the Rüden gild (aristocratic), who might treat to cakes at the birth of the first child, but no one should bring gifts on this occasion. (Figure 7.)

Social customs are thus incidentally revealed, as when the council of Zurich in 1680 saw a new evil rising in the giving of gloves to women who took part in such ceremonies. Forbidden under a rather heavy fine it appears again in an ordinance of 1691, but is not mentioned in 1697, and seems to be lost in the eighteenth century. Various devices were also framed to prevent circumventing the law by gifts to the mother, or interchange of presents among sponsors, temptation to which must have been strong on such occasions.

The strictness of most of these regulations continued through the eighteenth century, but with some relaxation in the entertainment of sponsors and relatives from a distance. In Basel in 1750 one carriage was permitted to carry the infant to and from the church, but at the same time the council complained that there had been great excess of expense for suppers and collations at congratulations, and

Fig. 7. Child-Bed Visit in Basel.

ordained that in future such entertainments with coffee, tea, confectionery, and the like must entirely cease. Yet the dining of the special participants had to go on, for in 1785 in Zurich the authorities struck at another practice in ordering that christening feasts should not be held in taverns, but in the house of the giver, where the fare must be modest; and no other "*Freudenfest*" was allowed beyond the meals served before and after the christening.

Birthday gifts to the child should be comparatively small, and must not exceed one ducat at the altar and one-half that amount up to the twelfth anniversary, with heavy penalty for excess of generosity. The latter motive was given room for play when the children of poor relatives were baptised, for there was practically no restriction in the help which might be extended at that time.

V. FUNERALS

THE regulation of funerals goes back into ancient history, and in view of the mediaeval conception of law we need not be surprised to find such rules existing in the seventeenth and eighteenth centuries. Such ordinances have evidently been long in operation, for definite acts of this kind were in force in the second half of the fourteenth century.

The most prominent motive in all this legislation is the desire to prevent superfluous expense, although minor regulations are often included to promote the peaceful conduct of such ceremonies. The natural desire in great grief to give all possible honor to the departed is sometimes supplemented by a subtler motive to provide a sumptuous funeral display. For either case city councils began early to set the limits for the funeral expense to which the relatives might go, in order to prevent the wealthy from overmuch outlay, and the poor from assuming costs which might for a long time imperil their economic welfare.

In Zurich the codes which cover the period from 1336 to 1374 required that at no funeral, whether the person be poor or rich, should there be more wax given than ten pounds, and this might be used for candles or otherwise. This limit was further maintained in that neither on the seventh day nor on the thirtieth day after the funeral should any one bring offerings of candles or other things to any church or cloister, under penalty of five pounds in money. If the mourners did not wish to use the cloth or pall furnished by the church for the bier, the friends might buy a silk cover, to cost not over one mark of silver. It was further ordered that no woman should give thanks to the people, standing in the church, or before it as many did. The ordinance affirmed in 1370 still more explicit directions on this point, saying further that this giving of thanks " is a form of luxury and of no benefit to the departed." Disobedience might bring on a fine or banishment from the city for one month.

26

Relatives might visit the grave as often as they wish but they also are forbidden to extend thanks in the church, nor might any gild visit the grave after the breakfast on the next day, " for this is no good to the soul of the departed." To assure peace to the mourners no one might go to the house except two friends or neighbors, and in this way every one might protect his house and his fires.

In Bern a century and a half later, in 1526, just before the Protestant Reformation, the amount of wax was still subject to regulation; but now it was fixed according to the rank of the deceased. For high officials there might be four candles of ten pounds, for lower nobility two candles of that weight. Lesser people might be honored according to the family means, but the weight of wax must not exceed five pounds. After the funeral the candles were to be divided between the church of the parish and the cathedral of St. Vincent.

The later history of this form of lawmaking shows a strong effort to limit the cost of funerals in two directions, one by fixing the number of guests allowed at a funeral dinner, and another by limiting the time and the number of persons who should wear mourning. This latter item included both the relatives and the servants of the house, to whom mourning garments had to be furnished.

The ordinance of Basel in 1677 attempted to shorten the exercises by ruling that the length of funeral speeches must be moderated. It was sufficient to have two or three relatives express sympathy in a few words, and these addresses were not to be extended by others. Funeral sermons must be shortened, especially in time of epidemic. The mourners might be accompanied to the grave, but the condolences might not begin there again; and since it is the custom to have the speeches in the pulpit after the sermon, it is super-fluous to have them again at the house. Covering walls with black cloth is extravagant, and in time of epidemic a dangerous practice, subject to a fine.

In 1661 extravagance in flowers, especially for young persons, was prohibited or fined, and it was noted further that at funerals of prominent persons people flock in and fill up the seats reserved for the mourners. Outsiders should go to the house and join the procession to the church in an orderly manner. Later on, by 1727, funeral rules had been reduced to a paragraph describing who may wear mourning, with the complaint that this matter has been too much extended with unnecessary expense. Consequently a list of those entitled to wear black was enacted, including husband or wife, parents, grandparents on either side, child, grandchild, son's

Fig. 8. Bern. Mourning Dress. 17th Century. By Conrad Meyer.

1. Married woman in church costume in mourning.
2. Married woman in church costume not in mourning.
3. Married woman, another mourning costume.
4. Married woman, another church costume.
5. Young lady in mourning.

wife, daughter's husband, brother, sister, brother or sister-in-law, etc. This enumeration was the same in 1769, except for a diminution of the fine. In that year mourning for step-relatives and the time limit for the ascending line was limited to one year, and for descending and side lines reduced to one-half year. The wearing of mourning by commercial and other servants was at the same time abolished. When the deceased had no near relatives the nearest might wear such clothing for one-half year. (Figure 8.) What further seems to be a good act was the complete abolition of condolences and funeral orations. The orator must begin at the fixed time with reading and nothing else, or pay a fine of ten pounds. As late as 1780 the restrictions remained the same, except that the fine for mourning outside the established rules was reduced from fifty to twenty pounds.

In Zurich in 1755 the ordinance shows distinctly the sumptuary principle involved. The wearing of mourning for parents, grandparents, husband, wife, or grandchildren, was limited to one year, while for more remote relatives the time was shorter and the dress limited to the so-called "small mourning." No attendants except house servants might wear funereal garments and that only for the head of the house, father or mother, and for the longest period they were to receive only one suit of black clothing. Up to the close of the century the laws remained fixed, with only slight varia-tions in the fines and time limits. In 1785 it was ordered that funeral meals should be held in the house of the family, not in a tavern, and only relatives and friends from out of town could be present. Other persons living in the same place must not join in this eating, while moderation in the expense of entertainment was expected.

In all three cities the ordinances were similar in controlling the ceremonies, and especially in regulating funeral meals and the extent to which relatives should participate in the outward signs of grief. The wearing of black for long periods may have been ostentatious, but the underlying trouble must have lain in cost, where whole families and servants must have new clothing, while the limitation of funeral dinners not only spared the feelings of the mourners but kept down the expense of entertainment. Into this latter subject city councils felt fully competent to enter.

The country districts gave the authorities much concern, on account of the crowds which customarily came together to take part in the ceremonies and to partake of the funeral baked meats. Ordinances were issued, but the matter was difficult to control where friendly feeling might abound throughout a whole township.

As to the efficiency of these ordinances, the writer has little positive evidence to show whether they were well obeyed in their early history. For the late seventeenth and the eighteenth centuries the court records show that the people were either extremely obedient or that the authorities were reluctant to prosecute cases arising from funerals. In the docket of the Reformation-Chamber of Basel covering this period their absence is noteworthy. Taking some twenty different years where the activity of the tribunal was vigorous, there were no citations for the infraction of ordinances strictly regulating funeral ceremonies. Among the prosecutions for dress some offenses may have occurred at a funeral, but we are not so informed, nor do funeral feasts appear as such, although both of these subjects continued to have their place in the law.

In Zurich, where the court record covers all but a few years of the eighteenth century, there was only one case brought up, and that was a mistake. In 1787 at a funeral there appeared sixteen bearers instead of the lawful eight, and the gild which they represented was called before the court. The answer was that the gild had provided the extra eight without expense to the family, and the case was dismissed.

VI. WEDDINGS

E VER since the days of Solon the regulation of weddings has been considered a function of government, so we need not feel surprised to find such laws early in the history of the cities of Switzerland. The religious side of the question is not under consideration here. The church provided the regulations concerning the relationship of the parties and the ceremonies by which the union was confirmed. Under the Roman Catholic régime the act was considered a sacrament, and under Protestantism a matter so sacred that obedience to the law must be complete, both in order to be right in the sight of God and to establish the rights of property and inheritance which ensued from such a union. Our interest in this matter lies in the regulations provided for the secular celebration of the marriage act, which are sumptuary almost without exception. Restraint upon the festivities of such occasions seemed to be necessary, and while the reason is often expressed that excess is unpleasing in the sight of the Almighty, the economic motive is strongly in evidence. The desire to avoid great expense upon this joyous occasion is easily understood, and the impulse to extravagance comes from the wish to do and provide as much as other weddings offer, and even to outshine others in generosity. Authorities felt compelled to intervene in the interest of economy and to set the limits beyond which bridal couples might not go in such celebrations. To obtain these ends in the three cities which we have under view, the ordinances bear a great similarity, hence selections from the laws of each have been made which show the changes which occurred as time advanced, and which reflect the customs and manners of the seventeenth and eighteenth centuries.

The chief topics which gave concern to the lawmakers were, first, the number of people who might be invited to take part in the ceremonies and join in festivities which followed, then the expense of the gifts which might be received by the new couple, especially from people who were not close relatives, and, finally, the number of musicians who might be hired to take part in the occasion. These things meant expense to the bridegroom, or to the father of the family, which might prove a burdensome economic excess. Likewise, other provisions which were added or taken away from time to time usually had to do with the prevention of extravagance.

In Zurich as early as 1304 such regulations appeared in the ordinances of the city council. At that time the bride and the bridegroom might each invite ten married ladies, not counting the bridesmaids and children who might be there. There must be only one wedding dinner, and no other citizen could be invited to the table. No one should give more than one present to the bride, either at the announcement of the engagement, at the wedding, or as a gift on the morning after, nor could the bride or bridegroom give or exchange gifts with any of their friends. No wedding procession could have more musicians than two singers, two fiddlers, and two trumpeters. The only exception to the law is that guests who come from outside the city need not be included in this rule of numbers.

Similar rules were enacted from time to time during the fourteenth century. In 1374 the musicians might be increased to ten, but the bride or groom must refrain from giving food to other musicians, a device intended to prevent excess of artists, either by invitation or as hangers-on. In 1400 complaint was made that a new custom had arisen, where the bridegroom gave a dinner to the people who sent him gifts and stood by him. This might be done in moderation, but no bridegroom should send food to any society or gild. In 1529 the regret is again expressed that weddings have become more and more extravagant. Guests are therefore limited to twenty-four, or if the relatives are very numerous, forty may be invited, and persons coming without an invitation are subject to a fine. Dancing at weddings is forbidden, as it was likewise in 1531, for "dancing is unseemly and awakens the wrath of God," who takes note of the sins of mankind by sending hard times, epidemics of death, and terrifying comets. Dancing could take place at other times, but when too boisterous it must be stopped. Persons were appointed to watch over this part of a festal program.

In Basel on February 23, 1628, a special wedding ordinance was passed which decreed that there must be no more gift weddings and no more wedding dinners in private houses. These must be held in a gild house or a public inn, where numbers and arrangements could be observed. Guests were limited to four tables of twelve as before, and the same year it was further enacted that such dinners were to be held on Mondays only. If ordered for Tuesday the fine would be two gulden, and an additional *Nachtessen* was liable to a penalty of twenty.

A full list of a course dinner was included as a sample to be followed in the matter of cost. Nothing more expensive was to be allowed, and one may safely say that the appetite of the party could be fairly well satisfied.

Entrées (*Als zu Eingang.*)
1. Head and cress or chopped mutton. (Later: " or roast pig.")
2. Soup two plates.
3. Two chickens with beef, veal, and smoked meat.
4. Cabbage, turnips, or peas according to season.

Second Course.
One plate large fish, or two plates small fish.

Third Course.
1. Two plates veal and one mutton or roast lamb.
2. Pigeons or cockerels, two plates.
3. Rice or " Bride's mush," two small plates.
4. Plums or pears.

Dessert (*Nachtisch.*)
Cheese, butter, goat-cheese, fruit according to season, *gofren* or wafers. (Later amended: " or a plate of cakes according to choice.")

Dinner must begin at 12 o'clock, stop at 4, and everybody leave by 5 o'clock. The cost of the repast must not exceed 22 *plappart* for a man, 18 for a woman, and 16 for a girl, but less can be arranged.

(*Plappart* about one shilling.)

The general mandate of 1637 in Basel devotes sixteen duodecimo pages to weddings, and from this a good report may be obtained of what occurred on such an occasion, for this ordinance enters into more particulars than most of its predecessors. As to the ceremony, the procession must be at the church punctually at nine o'clock in the morning, before the clergyman enters the pulpit, and he is not obliged to wait. Congratulations must not interfere with the movement of the party, nor shall any " May parties " or expensive pageantry with flowers or other pressure of people hinder the prompt arrival at the altar. A bridegroom who is late must pay a fine of one mark, and sextons must give the crowd due warning or lose their jobs. At the stroke of nine the bell was to be rung, and all must be assembled as quickly as was customary at other services. The whole wedding party was expected to be present during the service and sermon, for which a time limit is not specified.

The wedding dinner was held in an inn or gild house, and the bridal pair with the guests must be on hand and sit down at twelve o'clock. Disorders have arisen from late dinners, sometimes delayed till one o'clock, which is " *verdriesslich* " to guests and causes painfully long sitting. If the delay is due to the caterer, and the courses are not served at the time fixed, he is subject to a fine of one mark in silver. The last course must be put on at three, all drink orders must stop at four, and at five everybody must rise from the table. After that, young people were allowed any amusements except dancing, but if the wedding took place on the eve of a holy day all must go directly home.

The authorities were much concerned over the expense of wedding feasts, which not only consume and increase the cost of the provisions of the city and the country, but set the young couple, their parents and even their guests in embarrassment and trouble, especially the bridal pair, who at the very beginning of marriage are placed in debt, impatience, and even in diminution of property and food. Hence restriction of guests to forty-eight and the regulation of the dinner program. The menu was only slightly changed from that of

1628, with a view of shortening the time, preventing long
sitting, superfluous drinking, and some expense to the host.
Drinks must be paid for at each table, and only the clergyman and the master of ceremonies (*Braut-führer*), are entitled to free entertainment. Only one meal may be given on
the wedding day, and a fine is set for giving a luncheon or
supper on the next day, as well as for further eating or

Fig. 8a.   Zurich.   Bride, 1649.
By Wenzel Hollar.

drinking when the party giver came around to settle with
the tavern keeper. The "customary" coming together for
a "wine-warming" or the sending out of such refreshment
is likewise forbidden. The matter of wedding gifts is stated
with a brevity and certainty that would relieve the mind and
pocket-book of a modern reader. (Figure 8a.)

"Therefore we ordain and establish herewith that in
future all and every wedding with gifts, and likewise all
wedding gifts and presents (except what may be given by

parents or close relatives) are absolutely and entirely done away with, forbidden, and abolished (*abgeschafft, verboten, und aufgehoben*)."

Men and women must appear at the dinner in the sober garments prescribed for church services, and not let pride tempt them to change to a more festive secular costume. This rule evidently encountered the pressure of fashion and the desire of women to look their best at a wedding, for by 1715 it is distinctly announced that ladies sometimes change into four different dresses, powder their hair, wear low-cut jackets, short and multicolored undergarments, and white costly aprons. These offensive changes of costume must cease, and after wearing the black church habit through the ceremony they may change but once into colored dress, and continue thus to the end of the festivities.

The ordinance of 1637 contains various other regulations about the place young men should take in the procession either alongside of married men, or if together they must walk quietly, indicating that youthful pranks might occur. Rules fixed the details of the dinner without affecting the sumptuary outlay, or curbed any attempt to circumvent the ordinance by treats of another name. Regretting once more the growing expense of public dinners, the council admonished officials to observe moderation, and abolished until further notice all congratulatory banquets to elected councillors, judges, academic doctors, and the like, owing to " these troublous times." These troublous times were in the later phases of the Thirty Years' War, which although it did not enter Switzerland, devastated central Europe and affected badly the economic conditions of the neighboring countries.

Three-quarters of a century later the ordinance of 1715 reaffirms the previous rules, but contains some new orders on wedding gifts. The cost of rings must not exceed 150 *reichsthaler*, and a gold chain for the bride is limited to fifty or sixty *kronen* in weight. The gift from the father-in-law or mother-in-law may be a modest gold ornament, but no gold chain, ring, or other jewel. Gifts from bride and groom have been much overdone, hence are totally forbidden. This official admission is significant when we recall that for more than a century the laws had attempted to stop or regulate return gifts to relatives, evidently in vain. Wedding guests must also restrain their ornamentation, for no woman may appear in neck band of pearls or precious stones, or with clasps of precious stones, and single girls may wear only a gold chain of ten or fifteen *kronen* weight.

Most of the regulations of ceremonies and festivities were repeated, but with the complaint again that daily evidence showed the extravagance of wedding dinners. The number of guests, including relatives and all others, was now fixed at thirty-six, and no more might attend the ceremony. Stewards of gilds or inns must report the number to the Reformation Court. Dancing, however, is now allowed at these parties and may continue till eleven at night. A practice not considered in the early ordinances is here found in the rule that bringing guests in coaches, or carriage riding in or out of the city on such occasions is totally forbidden, as an abuse which has been creeping in of late, along with extra dinners for the master of ceremonies, collations, cakes, and confectionery, which increase the cost of getting married. (Figure 9.)

By 1736 the number of guests is raised to fifty, and continues the same to the end of the century. Dancing may be enjoyed, and the time limit extended from eleven o'clock to twelve, but must not take place in private houses unless in honor of a master of ceremonies, with only three musicians. In 1742 a revulsion of feeling caused the council to forbid dancing entirely at weddings and sleighride parties, but in a few years they returned to the rule that this amusement could take place only on these occasions. The law against carriages also evidently met popular opposition, for the ordinance of 1769 permits a full citizen (*Burger*) to provide eight coaches for his wedding, and the dependent resident (*Hintersass*) may have two.

In Zurich in the eighteenth century the regulations were similar to those of the other two cities, although the dates of changes may be different. Control of processions, shooting

Fig. 9. Wedding, 1751. By David Herrliberger.

of guns, and disturbances in general point to habits which were likely to manifest themselves anywhere on these joyful occasions, the restraint of which would not be necessary unless they actually happened.

The limitation of guests appears throughout, and the authorities of Zurich were anxious over the rural population, where the number of participants was moved up to forty or sixty, but the invitation of whole communities or townships was strictly forbidden. One can see that the temptation was very strong in the country to include a whole neighborhood, not only in order to please all friends, but to keep up with, or exceed, the social demands of such an occasion. The bad economic results of such expenditure were obvious without the lines of complaint and warning in the ordinances. In all of these places the effort was made to confine the festivities to one day, sometimes fixing the day of the week on which marriages could take place, and further to prevent the sending out of drink treats to people not on the list of guests, or stop providing suppers on the day following (*Nach-hochzeiten*), all of which added to the expense of the wedding.

Summarizing in a general way the evidence of the records of Zurich for a century after 1304, where these studies begin, wedding givers might entertain twenty guests. During the next two centuries the limit rose to forty or sixty, and continued to be confined to relatives or very close friends. In Basel in the first half of the seventeenth century the ordinances permitted forty-eight guests at the ceremonies and dinners. An attempt to reduce this number to thirty-six in 1715 apparently was not popular, for a few years later the count was changed to fifty, and thus remained to the end of the century.

When the court records of the eighteenth century are examined, the prosecutions for disobedience to the wedding ordinances are infrequent and far apart. Between 1687 and 1795 in Basel there are periods in the dockets from one to ten years in length where no cases are recorded, and when on record the trials rarely number more than one a year,

Fig. 10.   Zurich Family, 1643.   Grace before Meat.

although prosecutions for other sumptuary offenses are numerous. Much the same can be said for Zurich in the same period, where very few citations appear for excess in dinners, one or two a year for shooting, a few more for dancing, some for unlawful clothing or jewelry, and perhaps one for a guest who was not a relative. The complaints of neglect and disobedience, with which almost every new ordinance begins or repeats, do not let us suppose that whole communities were in fear of these laws, even when the threats of prosecution were reiterated every few years during more than two centuries.

VII. CLOTHING. 1370 TO 1600

ORDINANCES respecting costume and personal decoration appear in the records of the fourteenth century, but hardly go beyond the admonition to avoid extravagance, and they give few particulars as the dress which may or may not be worn. Sharp restrictions belong to the second period of this study, and continue to the French revolution, sumptuary legislation being persistent and sometimes exacting in its requirements. The steady continuation of such ordinances, showing the constant urge to make regulations on these subjects, and the evidence respecting the diligence exhibited in the enforcement of them are topics which throw interesting light upon the social conditions of the time.

In this connection the oft-repeated reasons for sumptuary laws must be brought to mind. One of the first avowed motives is personal economy and the avoidance of expenditure upon superfluous clothing and ornamentation. This is a logical derivative from the paternal conception of government prevailing in those times. Furthermore, the ordinances provide restrictions in the amount which different classes of the population may spend, sometimes pointing out with great particularity the limits within which the various ranks must confine themselves. The difference, to be sure, is based upon the spending power of the different classes, since servants would not have the resources of their masters or civic superiors; but the law is also founded upon the avowed principle of distinction in rank, which must also show itself in distinction in clothing. The statement is often openly expressed that servants attempt to imitate their superiors, and that no one can tell by the looks of the people the difference in classes. Again the laws seem to maintain a persistent animosity against changes in fashion. In addition to motives of economy there is a desire to maintain a strictly national costume against the invasion of foreign materials and foreign

42

fashions, the patriotic emotion being frequently called in to strengthen the law, while persons coming into the country to reside are given a limit of time to conform to the local costume. Other minor motives may have been included, but the reasons already given are sufficient to explain the continued attempt to control the outer appearance of fellow citizens.

The regulation of the clothing to be worn in church is more or less an evident duty under the circumstances, since the service is a dignified religious ceremony. Likewise, the dress to be worn at christenings is based upon a principle fully understood in that period, although we may wonder at the minutiae often shown in describing permissible garments.

In following these laws through some three centuries, and noting that at various times a most vigorous onslaught is made upon existing fashions, we have to realize that in spite of everything fashions did change. Compared to the present day, patterns of dress were slow in changing, but transformations did take place; so that while we are considering the law at a given date we must also call to mind the costume of the hour.

The laws themselves lend aid to this task, and portraits of the times must be drawn upon to show the things against which the ordinance might be directed. Following the matter further we find that the costume of the middle and upper classes throughout Europe is similar, and shows differences only in minor details in each group. When we look further for the cause of all this we shall find that in the seventeenth and eighteenth centuries France is the arbiter of fashion, and this leadership includes both the garments and a host of their common names. We shall find, in short, that this is a contest between the lawmaker and the dressmaker, the outcome of which will in a measure appear as we proceed with this narrative.

The earliest law from which we may gather a description of the fashions of the times is an ordinance passed in Zurich about 1370. In order to appreciate the objections of the lawmakers we shall need to picture to ourselves a man dressed in a tight-fitting suit, the jacket coming down somewhere toward his knees, and on his head a cap or hood, with a tail anywhere from three feet long till it touched the ground. The lady also wore a dress fitting closely to her form above the waist, but reaching with ample cloth to the ground, with possibly a trail. The use of bright colors was common in the dress of both sexes, so that the man with his pointed shoes

Fig. 11.   Fourteenth Century.

and his long hood and the lady with long tails to her sleeves and low neck to her dress would easily attract the attention which the wearer desired. (Figure 11.)

To counteract the tendency to over-ornamentation the Council of Zurich about 1375 ordered that no woman, whether married, widow, or ecclesiastic, should put embroidery on any cloth, veil, silk, or linen, but should leave it as first woven. There must be no crown headdress decorated with gold, silk, or precious stones, nor should any hood have any such ornaments; but at the same time girls and young women were permitted to have these things on their head-dresses. In earlier times women's dresses were loose, and when put on were drawn over the head. Now with tighter garments it was necessary to have them open in front and fastened with buttons, but here the council stepped in and decreed that every woman should have a dress so close-fitting in the neck that the opening would be only two inches on the shoulders. No buttons or lacing were allowed on this gar-ment, and except for young women it should have no gold, silver, or jewels. Hoods sometimes reached the ground, but the law said the tail should not exceed one ell in length. The dress must be all of one color, and the girdle or belt must not cost more than five pounds. Pointed shoes were forbidden for any person, and women must not have foot-wear fitted with lacing strings. Men and boys must have their outer garment reach to the knees, and the tail of the hood must be of the same length as the coat and not be slashed. Trouser legs must not be striped nor made of cloth of different colors, and a rather heavy penalty was attached to disobedience to any or all of these injunctions.

About a century later, in 1488, the authorities of Zurich were still complaining at the prevalence of costly clothing, so they said again that no woman should wear any silver or gold-plated pins, rings, or buckles. They must avoid silk garments or silk trimmings on coats, shoes, neckcloths, and such like, unless they belonged to the aristocratic gilds, the *Rüden* and *Schnecken*. No woman was to have a belt with metal mountings unless her husband had an income of a thousand gulden or over, and then it must not cost more than twelve gulden. Women of this class might have silk borders on their bodices, but without hooks or buckles. (Figure 12.) The penalty for non-observance of this rule was confiscation of the belt; or the authorities might be compelled to sell it for the benefit of the husband's business necessities. As a social indication it might be noted that these forbidden ornaments are allowed to public prostitutes and no others.

In Bern in 1464 the community was startled by the robbery of sacred vessels from the church, and this was taken as a

sign of the displeasure of Providence. Consequently the
authorities ordered, among other things, that extravagance
in clothing should be curbed, and in particular decreed that
the prevailing short coats and mantles were shameful exhi-
bitions of the person, and must be made to cover the middle
of the body. Shoes could have points no longer than one
finger, or the wearer or maker would be liable to a fine of

Fig. 12.   Fifteenth Century.

ten shillings and banishment for one month. Women's
dresses might trail on the ground not more than the span of
one hand.

Six years later, after strife with the nobility which came
almost to civil war, the length of trains was reaffirmed, but
exceptions were made in favor of noble ladies, who might
have gold and precious jewels on their breasts, headdresses
and elsewhere, as well as gold or other neck ornaments, all
of which would distinguish them from the ordinary women.
These latter had been imitating the upper classes too much,

and were ordered not to wear parti-colored fur, marten, or ermine on their clothing.

Clear to the end of the fifteenth century ordinances were directed against the wearing of short garments, but the trouble went over into the next century and was aggravated by an intense desire on the part of the male population to wear clothing decorated with slashes. This fashion was a product of the Renaissance, and flourished in an atmosphere which gave birth to fine works of art and architecture. Jackets, breeches, and sleeves were covered with long cuts, under which puffs of cloth, perhaps of another color, were inserted; and the whole costume presented a striking appearance, and in spite of it all was really artistic. The fashion was fostered in Switzerland by the mercenary soldiers returning home, yet for various reasons the authorities took offense at this display. (Figure 13.) In Bern, for example, a memorandum to the Great Council called attention to the presence of slashed clothing in one of the outer districts. In 1530 the wearers of trousers thus cut at the knee were in future to be punished, and garments of any kind were not to be cut or slashed in any way after the coming Easter. At this same session one John Mischler was brought before the court for having his breeches slashed at the knee. In reply he stated that this garment had become too small and he was obliged to cut it open to make it fit. The excuse prevailed and the fine was remitted, but the fashion went on.

The changes which took place toward the end of the fifteenth century are set forth in great detail in the chronicle of Bern of 1503, written by Valerius Anselm, who was evidently a pessimistic devotee of old times, but he favors us with a picture of costume which shows with what factors in fashion the conservative authorities felt obliged to contend.

After a general complaint over the decay of Swiss simplicity and honesty, Anselm points out changes in dress and manners which had taken place during the previous ten years. Omitting his descriptions of garments formerly worn and noting only his references to contemporary costume, it appears that men had become so extravagant that they were to be seen in shag hats, storm barettes, and wore cloth from St. Gall and even from London and Lombardy. Their long coats and mantles had many folds and broad shapes, and there were inner and outer dress coats as well as coats with

Fig. 13.   Swiss Soldier, 16th Century, after Holbein.

wide half-sleeves. Waistcoats of cotton had stiff woolen broad collars with wide breast pieces, were cut out on the shoulder, and ornamented with silver buttons back and front. Silk jackets were in favor — even the peasants had begun to wear silk. Trousers had high fastenings, and there were great lined waistcoats, and whole stockings divided in colors

from the top downward. Shirts were built in folds with wide
openings and trimmed with ribbons. Men went about in
breeches and jacket, a habit formerly considered a great
shame. Their shoes were blunt and had wide perforations,
either with or without rings, and even slippers appeared in
public.

After a long list of fancy weapons, evil games, costly
foods, and other extravagences, the author remarks that the
yellow color formerly called "Judas" has become the com-
monest of tints, one shade of which is already known as
"Swiss Yellow" (*Schweizergelb*).

Women's costume at this time included large lined silk
ribbons braided into the hair and high bushy hoods, while
yellow cloth raised or ornamented with borders was used for
neck and breast covering. They wore many lockets, with
collars of good cloth trimmed with silk, or silk goods embroidered with silk, a fashion which reached even into the
stable and kitchen. Jackets and smocks were either loose or
close-fitting, and had long narrow sleeves bordered with silk.
(Figure 14.) Petticoats were worn in many folds and in
different colors, were slitted at the elbows, and had wide
embroidery of special tints. Belts with clasps, long earrings,
little knives with hammered ornamentation, fat purses with
buttons, or without buttons, little shoes, boots and slippers
with perforations, red in color and ending in blunted toes;
all these were in evidence.

Everything that loose women brought in from the wars
and from foreign lands along with their luxuriousness, and
what the artistic painters portrayed in the churches, came to
such high honor that even the nunneries took them on, and
they have become so common that prostitutes and painters
have nothing to do but think of something new. As these
costly habits have increased, so also have increased envy,
covetousness, cunning, unfaithfulness, unbelief, pride, luxury,
and contempt. With them all gainful arts have sharply ex-
panded, especially those which serve the tongue, and the
handwork which ministers to luxurious pride, such in particular as painters, goldsmiths, silk embroiderers, stone-

masons, glass-cutters, seamstresses, cloth-workers, singers, and musicians. Likewise, there is much shopkeeping, along with selfish merchant associations, many idlers, window sports, soldiers, whores, and all kinds of knaves, of whom

Fig. 14. Swiss Costume. 16th Century.
After Holbein.

the majority and the most prominent are respected and esteemed as well-ordered, witty, honest, and upright people.

This fierce indictment has a certain measure of justification, coming as it does at a time when the mercenary service of the Swiss was bringing a serious deterioration of moral habits. Money received from foreign countries in the pockets of soldiers and officials was indeed leading to luxury, but judgment may be suspended respecting the extent to which the people as a whole were led into corruption. For the moment the changes of fashion are the matters for consideration.

In 1537 it was ordered that announcement be made from the pulpit that citizens would be given a period of one week in which they must remove their slashes and sew up the openings. In 1541 the pulpit was again requested to call attention to slashed clothing, and thus it went on, letters and resolutions appearing every few years, and even in the so-called Great Ordinance of 1573, along with warnings against immodest and extravagant and foreign clothes, the only garments specifically named were the time-honored slashed breeches.

It should not be assumed that during all this time all men wore slashed clothing. Introduced from abroad during the Renaissance it became particularly popular, but a glance at the portraits of the period show that other forms of costume were in use, and the vivid colors and spectacular cuts gradually gave way to new fashions. (Figure 14a.) The long contest with the conservatism of the law indicates the slowness of change and the persistence of modes which little by little disappear from the prohibitions of city councils.

It would be difficult to divide sumptuary legislation into fixed limits of time, for some of it remains throughout the whole period, and fashions pay no attention to advances in the calendar. It is safe to say, however, that the surviving laws from the seventeenth century enter into greater particularity respecting the whole costume and the articles which the citizen may or may not wear. From the prohibitions and exceptions we may not be able to draw a picture complete in all details of the men and women who walked the streets or entered the churches of the cities, but we may obtain a vivid idea of many things which people were wearing, for the almost violent language of the law would not have been employed by the city councils if they had not seen the objectionable fashions in actual use.

The paternal responsibility felt by lawmakers for their

fellow citizens lost none of its power as the government during this period became more and more aristocratic. The attempt to distinguish classes through the cost and quality of their garments would lose none of its strength with the

Fig. 14a.   Hans Jacob Schwyzer.
Zurich, 1564.
By Tobias Stimmer.

upper classes in power, as they looked down upon the subordinate orders. The superiority of the governing classes in political matters is decidedly evident, but we shall see as we proceed in how far they were successful in regulating personal appearance.

VIII. CLOTHING. SEVENTEENTH CENTURY

ANOTHER matter which gives us the power to see genuine economic principles now involved in their sumptuary legislation is the fact that during the first half of the seventeenth century the greater part of Europe was shattered and almost paralyzed by the Thirty Years' War. Switzerland was not involved in the military strife of this contest, but, although the country was better off than many others, it suffered much from military disturbance. When the preambles of the ordinances call attention to the " evils of these times " and urge the necessity of restraint or the avoidance of extravagance in living, the reasons are sound, although we may not agree with the feasibility of the restrictions which were actually imposed in the laws. While economy may be only one of the reasons for attempting to regulate personal expenditure, we are bound to give it respect so far as it goes.

The sumptuary laws of these towns, fuller of detail than heretofore and based upon the same fundamental principles, display a certain similarity, but they are rarely simultaneous in date, and in their particulars show variety of locality. Selections will be made from different places, in the attempt to show how far they reached into the private life of the community.

An ordinance of Zurich in 1610 repeats the well-worn complaint that no one is obeying the law, while there is much extravagance in clothing and living, and no one is dressed according to his rank and condition. Great coats supported within by wicker work expanding the same from the body were in vogue, while women and girls were wearing coats like those of the men. Great built-up breeches recently appearing on men must not be worn, nor any silk mantles, nor gold or silver cords on expensive silk or velvet garments. Great ruffs, sometimes double or treble or too long, must cease, or the penalty of five marks in silver will be imposed upon any breach of these regulations.

In all of these cities clothing regulations were frequently

renewed, and we shall need to select from them prominent
ones which display the tendencies of the time. The ordinance
of Bern of 1628 is one of these, and we shall have to understand that the civic costume of that town had changed, but
still both men and women were given to elaborate decoration
of their clothing, much to the concern of the city authorities.
The knee-breeches were still there, but coats were somewhat
changed in form, and we can gather from the law even without the portraits many of the items of which the dress of both
sexes was composed.

The Bern ordinance of 1628 begins with an admonition to
everybody to appear in clothing with all modesty and avoid
all superfluous and useless cost. Especially they must avoid
a multitude of cords lying close together on their clothing,
and should have their waistcoats, breeches, and sleeves made
of cloth or woolen suitable to the class to which the wearer
belonged. All men, young or old, were warned against the
large wide breeches which hang below the knee, as well as
narrow trousers adorned with lace, which had lately appeared. Likewise, the new form of waistcoat with long
Spanish lace, broad thick shoulders, or any adorned with
slashes with silk bands and ribbons on the sleeves and back,
the indecent ornaments used especially on vests, or below on
the breeches. In these hard times the common man must
beware of all costly things such as velvet, satin, silk, and
similar materials. Persons of quality and citizens of property
who wish to use that kind of material may have one or two
of the permitted cords on the seams of their waistcoats, and
along the folds of their breeches may place three, four, or,
at the most, five small cords. Although they are allowed to
have slashed or cut taffetas, or satin garments with silk material beneath, yet the cut must be made simple without excess
of insolent pride. Further, old men and young were forbidden to have upstanding, broad, misshapen mantle-collars
with their trimmings which have recently come into fashion,
nor yet the little mantles with gold or silver cords, passa-
menterie, or stripes at the side or underneath. In future the
mantle-collars must not be wider than one-quarter of an ell.

Also forbidden are the "hideous" great long thick ruffs on man or woman, old or young. One thickness only, or at the most double in respectable medium size will be allowed, but for servants, single only. (Figure 15.) All prominent men who are entitled to the privilege may have trimmings

Fig. 15.   Felicitas von Karpfen—Effinger, 1602.

on their arms three fingers wide without lace, and honorable women and daughters, four fingers wide including the lace. Servant maids are forbidden to wear these at all.

The fashions in hair were hard hit, and the authorities did not spare words in their description. Men were forbidden to appear in unbecoming, superfluous, great thick curled hair. Women must not wear their hair standing high up in wanton fashion, and were forbidden to have their sleeves slashed, or perforated, or decorated with ribbons, or have superfluous wide trimmings on these or their dress collars. Forbidden also were the use of fur, extra wide shoulders, long laces and braids on their sleeves, as well as the strange new trim-mings then coming in. Obedience was to be enforced by a respectable fine.

An ordinance of Basel in 1637 gives even more particulars regarding dress which may be permitted or forbidden. The subject occupies nearly twenty small pages, and from the contents there may be obtained a still more emphatic state-ment of class distinction. In its warnings against luxury, which were interspersed with expressions like "in these times" we are reminded that the Thirty Years' War was still in progress.

This ordinance devotes much space to the enumeration of jewelry, either forbidden or permitted, and leads one to think that no possible use of these ornaments could have been omitted. Women of all classes are told to avoid gold and half-gold embroidery, passementerie trimmings, cords, lace, embroidery, gold, silver, pearls or precious stones anywhere on their clothing, waistcoats, trimmings, girdles, shoes, slip-pers, rosettes (on headdress), garters, ribbons, and so on. Nor may they have hatbands of gold or half-gold, or any-thing ornamented with gold, silver, or precious stones. No one of any class except at musters or authoritative occasions may wear gold ornamented arms, velvet scabbards, or cloth-ing with the more expensive cords and passementerie em-broidery, made in such a way that the material of the articles cannot be seen. No camisoles made of taffeta or satin with mingled gold and silver may be included in their clothing.

"In these troublous times" men and women are to avoid chains of pearls, or wear openly gold chains, necklaces, or bracelets. Garments ornamented with pearls, such as ruffs, shirts, handkerchiefs, napkins, headdresses, pendant buttons, neckcloths, are not to be worn. In general all that kind of decoration, superfluous button-work upon linen, neck-mantles, oversleeves, flounces, and the like is forbidden, and every one is urged to avoid such unnecessary luxury.

Coming to clothing itself men, young or old, married or single, are forbidden to wear the "recently arrived filthy long *alla modo* breeches," or the wide ill-formed mantle-collars, as well as the "indecent, superfluous long hair," hair-locks hanging over the eyes, likewise false curled hair, "called Peruques," and in general they are earnestly warned to be clothed in the old Swiss, patriotic and German manner and to avoid completely foreign forms and costume.

All people are warned to use as little as possible of costly goods, such as satin, velvet, damask, and such like, for although these materials are not forbidden to those qualified to wear them, yet such people should set a good example to the lower classes and thus lead them to obedience and honesty.

Silk mantles and such as are lined with silk or similar costly stuff, or lined with expensive fur, marten, "romanisch," or trimmed outside with four or more silk borders, or with passementerie, all are forbidden to persons not qualified by birth or condition to wear them.

Women, "who, sad to say," are most given to luxury and expense, which daily increases, were warned to obey these rules or suffer disgrace and punishment. Those who were allowed to wear satin, damask, taffeta, silk, and similar costly stuffs (except sheared and unsheared velvet and linen (*caffa*) hereby prohibited) were forbidden to have on their damascene or silk sleeves or jackets, or on these when made of similar costly goods, any *satin* embroidered cords, but might have four or not more than five *silk* cords set simply one after the other along the border and not made into a pattern or fancy ornamentation. On coats of cloth or other materials not more than five borders or small cords might be set, and these must not be over one-third of an ell high, but rather lower.

In general it was forbidden to wear the "disgusting, superfluous" borders, "*Krägen*," or wide cuffs on sleeves, collars, and jackets, which hang down to the waist. These must not be more than one-third of an ell wide. Persons of quality might have fringes on their jackets and coat collars, but for others this was prohibited. This class was permitted to have five silk cords set on the collar, but no stitched satin cords except some on the hood.

Women of all classes must put off the all too short clothing as disgraceful and vexatious. The bosom must not be too wide open, but, according to the fashion which came down from old times, must be made somewhat closer. The scarfs or neck mantles must not be so small that they do not cover the trivial spirit of the wearer, but made the proper length in accordance with decency.

Concerning costly furs, the ordinance forbids sable for anybody. Women of the upper class might have marten as a lining for sleeves and collars, but they must use moderation to avoid sharp action from the authorities. Quality is permitted to wear fur trimming and may place on this borders of damask, taffeta, or other goods not more expensive, but the borders must not be too high, and the lower classes must not use this trimming at all. The "immense, disgusting" great fur hoods, the cost of which increases from day to day, were ordered stopped, with the interpretation that prominent women may wear velvet caps made with otter and other similar furs, provided the cost with all belongings was not more than twelve gulden. (Figure 16.)

Persons of rank and other prominent citizens were permitted to have gold rings and precious stones, but they must wear these with modesty so that nothing else will be charged against them. They were allowed solid silver on their swords, belts, buttons, sword hilts, etc., and might have white silverwork up to twelve or fifteen ounces. Wives and children could have solid silver or gilded chain belts, and might use on knives, sheaths, chains up to ten or fifteen ounces of that metal.

Men of any age or class were ordered to avoid the large, wide foreign coat collars "never seen here before" with their costly long laces, and with them must go the "detestable" long, thick ruffs. Exceptions were made for persons in the government and for prominent citizens with their wives and children, who might wear ruffs of Netherlands and foreign linen, but these must be of medium thickness and size. Men might have their single or multiple ruffs waved or drawn up with the finger, but women were allowed more freedom in the formation of this article, although they

Fig. 16. Swiss Headdress. 1679.

Frau Anna Salome Daxelhofer.

must avoid sumptuous excess. The multifold ruffs for either men or women must not exceed five-fold in thickness.

Men who were prominent in the city, especially government officials, and such as were from time to time in high position, or conspicuous citizens, might clothe themselves in fine English cloth, burat, grosgrain, and such goods, but were advised to do so in moderation, and not to set too much passementerie or cords upon vest and breeches, avoiding superfluity as much as possible.

Common citizens, small shopkeepers, artisans, and others of this class, with their wives and children, were to dress themselves in cloth costing not over three gulden an ell. They were forbidden to use velvet, satin, damask, taffeta, and such expensive goods except for mantle or sleeve collars. They must not wear good floret silk stockings, but might have on their breeches a simple line of passementerie, or a cord the width of a thumb. No sleeves or waistcoats of velvet were allowed, but for trimming on this garment they could have a small silk cord or a double stitching.

Neither they nor their families might use Netherland linen, only homespun (*Haustuch*) for their ruffs, and these must be made with the fingers, not with a crimper. They must not carry swords with solid silver ornamentation nor anything more costly, though six ounces of silver was permitted. No solid silver for wives and children. They must be content with silvered clasps with rough borders on belts, and on decorated knives and sheathes they could have six ounces of white silver.

Rings were forbidden entirely, except that the women could have gold rings without precious stones to be worn at weddings and other ceremonial occasions. Wives and daughters might wear upon their sleeves and jackets of permitted material only a stripe or two quiltings, and upon their dresses not more than three stripes one-quarter of an ell wide. They could have no *Romanisch* fur work, and their hats were to be made of inferior marten skin, while for hoods they must not spend more than six gulden including the making.

Women of this class were allowed to wear the daily house jacket (*Wammiss*), with moderation in the home in order that housekeeping might be more conveniently performed, but they must not appear in this on the street, and still less in church. With all due propriety the women according to ancient custom must appear at Sunday and Tuesday services in cloak and *tüchli*, and all of them, including maidservants, on the day when they have taken the holy communion should retain the *tüchli* until the evening.

Serving men, day laborers, their wives and children, seamstresses, ruff-makers, serving maids, and the like, must hereafter use for their clothing, whether it be for smocks, coats, jackets, bosoms, aprons, or anything else, only leather, corduroy, Lindisch or Basel cloth, Franckenthaler, double burail, and such like, or any material of lower cost. All other more expensive goods, like *trip-sammet* (mock-velvet), were entirely forbidden, even if received as a gift from their masters. Servant maids could have only one stripe on the dress, and that one-half an ell high, and the class as a whole could have no gold or silver on knives, belts, fittings, or clothing, no corals or other things around the neck, nor any imitation that gives the appearance of gold or silver. Ruffs for all this class must be made of common linen or *Haustuch* (homespun) and must not be over one-eighth of an ell long and fifteen ells thick, made simply and folded only by hand.

As to furs the ruff-makers, seamstresses, and maidservants were allowed black trimmings from sheepskin, and nothing more expensive was to be worn or used for sleevelinings. The women of all ordinary citizens were especially forbidden to wear swans-down about the neck.

For the women of the laboring class the price of hoods was limited to two gulden, to cover goods, lining, fur, and the cost of making. This class must not wear sewed hats, only simple felt, and must not appear in better ones, even if obtained as gifts or by inheritance. Peasant hats were to be worn plain with no cords on them, but they might be trimmed with small ribbons.

This labor group was restricted in the use of rosette ribbons, which cost more than one shilling an ell. Furthermore, it was emphatically forbidden to go about without a girdle, and this belt with its ornaments and the knife-sheath attached must not cost more than one pound. This class must not wear other stockings than those of cheaper cloth, or *Pariser Strümpf*, costing not more than eighteen *batzen* a pair, while their shoes should not be perforated, nor made of cordovan or velvet leather, but of common leather without heels.

The regulations in this ordinance respecting the dress to be used at wedding ceremonies may be called ceremonial and belong perhaps in the chapter on that subject, yet in reality they form a considerable part of the personal sumptuary rules thought necessary at that time. They provide a combination of law and fatherly advice, and at the risk of repetition certain features in this ordinance of 1637 should be noted.

Calling attention to the extravagances which occur on wedding occasions the council goes on to say that great superfluity has been observed, not only among persons of high standing, but also among common citizens and the artisan class, whereby they bring upon themselves serious debts, great injury, and destruction. Consequently the authorities desire that everyone conduct his affairs according to his rank and wealth, and avoid all unnecessary expense, so that they may not have cause to inflict punishment upon one or another. Especially forbidden are honorary gifts, bridal mementoes, and the like, which the bridal couple have hitherto provided for their friends and others most extravagantly so that they have become a social obligation. The laws attempt to stop all other destructive superfluities, such as the costly wedding ring which the bridegroom gives to the bride. " In the time of our forefathers " this was a plain wound ring, not one with precious stones costing many dollars, as has occurred with much vexation.

Although pearls, borders, and maiden ribbons have been customary from time past in this city, demanding great expense, and for that reason and perhaps others the total abolition would seem to be wise, yet for the time being we permit all unmarried girls to use these things as maiden ornaments, or, as is customary in other places, they may wear wreaths on their hats, along with the lawful dress or jacket; but in the matter of hats and wreaths a reasonable restraint must be used, and what has been introduced in one place must not become a misuse in another. On that account the daughters of persons of rank and otherwise noteworthy citizens are permitted to wear velvet hats with wreaths on them, but they must not be too costly. The daughters of artisans and the like are permitted to wear felt with thread-work. Seamstresses, ruff-makers, and maids may have felt, but with only a little thread-work in front.

In regard to ribbons and borders the following distinction must be kept in mind. The double kind are abolished, and only simple ribbons and borders may be worn. In future these may be made new for daughters of prominent people at a cost not over 200 pounds, and for others at not more than fifty or sixty pounds, under penalty of confiscation. As to wedding jackets, the daughters of highly prominent people may have an ell and one-half of velvet with fringes on the bosom; daughters of the artisan class two-thirds of an ell without fringes. In general and without distinction of persons it is entirely forbidden to wear over the jackets gold chains instead of belts, but it is permitted to daughters of prominent people only to wear ribbons and borders, yet they must not gird themselves with a whole or half gold braid or lace band.

If we are still in wonder at the minute regulations of dress it might be well to note that this is not the only field in which city councils issued their regulations. For instance, there was a code of prices issued in Basel in 1646 which occupies some seventy-seven pages in a duodecimo pamphlet. This code regulated seventy-eight different trades, all the way from apothecaries to wagon-makers. It included along with the regulation of the fees and service time of apprentices the prices of more than nine hundred and fifty commodities. These rules recite with great detail the articles made by the various kinds of artisans. Thirty-five different kinds of hats are listed; twenty-five kinds of shoes, besides the prices fixed for cobbler's repairs; the products of carpenters and coffin makers;—these are but samples of the code-fixing used in that period. Even the barbers were there, but their chief occupation was surgery, in which art all kinds of repairs to the human body from amputations and skull fracture down to simple blood-letting are enumerated in some thirty items. Finally, in about three lines at the bottom of the list, they cut hair at two shillings a head, or "break out" a tooth at the same price.

The ordinance of Zurich of 1636 complains of extravagance in housekeeping and clothing, and points back to the earthquakes as a warning quite similar to its contemporary of Basel of 1637. Misshapen long hair, thick ruffs, silver and gold embroidery, extravagant headdresses, costly jewelry, — all occupy the attention of the authorities and show that the fashions in the two cities were very much alike.

The dress regulations of Zurich in 1650 were almost the same as in 1636, but they take up the details of costume with greater particularity. Even babes in the cradle have too much spent on them, and maids are so well dressed that their position is not discernible. Extravagance has gone to such lengths in ostentation and cost that the council is compelled to act. Everyone must wear simple small ruffs appropriate to civic ordinances, and careful watch will be kept so that transgressors will be punished. Certain persons have been allowed to wear smooth collars, but they must not be ornamented with lace or other expensive materials. (Figure 17.)

From the long list of permitted and forbidden things the women of all clasess would have no difficulty in finding out what form of personal garment or ornamentation they should adopt. At various times it seemed best to regulate the form of dress most suitable to the clerical profession. From Zurich we may take as example from about 1670 the recommendations of the executive board for the improvement of the costume of this class.

It is evident that ministers and their families must appear in more sober garments than the rest of the community. From the long list of things which were regarded as improper and subject to censorship for men it was forbidden to have unseemly long hair, large loose hanging hat-bands, the new *Schis-kappen* or small hats, then coming into fashion, large collars on their coats, sword hangings with fringes, double buttons on their garments, perforations in their red wool shirts or shirt-sleeves, silk stockings, large costly garters, and, coming finally to the bottom of the costume, they must avoid long pointed shoes or large shoe-ribbons.

The women of the clerical families were provided with as many " don'ts " as the men, although some of the restrictions applied to all females. First, they must not wear the foreign Suabian hoods, nor large ears on the church headdress (*tüchli*), nor lace on their hoods. No ribbons under the chin, no triple collars, nor small neck-bands, which probably exposed the bosom, while perforated sleeves displayed the

Fig. 17. Basel. Woman, 1644.
By Wenzel Hollar.

arms. All kinds of lace on collars, headdresses or clothing must be avoided. The house dress must not be made of velvet, nor may they have the new kind of narrow aprons. No black gauze, no silver hooks, no costly clasps, and, in short, no expensive clothing of any kind were to be allowed.

These items are taken from a project of law offered by the small body appointed to enforce the sumptuary ordinances, and we can readily discern the attitude of the authorities and probably of the public in general toward the clergy who served them. They were expected not only to lead a righteous, upright life but to manifest their sober qualities in their outward appearance. The rules just given were not the only ones issued in the seventeenth century, and they all have a striking similarity, for the directions provided for the wives and children of the clergy in 1679 are almost the same as those of 1628.

Fig. 18.   Bern.   Costume about 1650.

By Wenzel Hollar.

The success of the authorities in enforcing their rules of dress can be seen in the minutes of a meeting of the Three Orders, comprising the heads of church government, the chamber of reformation and the matrimonial court, held on Sunday, August 20, 1671. After a list of complaints about Sabbath observance, attendance on Roman Catholic services, and various police matters, this body calls attention to troubles in the field of costume and records a series of objectionable innovations which have been creeping in.

It appears that Zurich ladies have not only been wearing forbidden gauze on their heads but also, on top of this, have been mounting little hats trimmed round and round with little ribbons that look like feathers. White sleeves are in use which open at the back and are drawn together with ribbons after the French manner. Sleeves also are made so short that the chemise must be bound twice around the arms with taffeta ribbons. Aprons in some cases are made very small or perhaps altogether omitted. Hair worn with flowing locks is a fashion coming into use, and objectionable hoods are seen trimmed with black ribbons. Sleeping caps are noted which have embroidered rosettes on both sides, and collars have ribbons decorated with pearls. Collars which are built up in five or more layers, may in fact be seen commonly in church in spite of ordinances and expense. Finally, they said that autumn farm labor on the Sabbath ought to be restrained. God was showing his anger in bad crops, and the matter was referred to the city council for more drastic action.

In 1672 in a communication to the council the Reformation-Chamber said that as to fluted collars it had hoped that its word of warning would put an end to them, but the longer the time the worse the habit. When the matter was brought to the attention of even the great people of the town it was answered that fluted collars were more useful than others, and in many households, especially where there are many daughters, this form was a noteworthy economy. The subject was left to the council, but a prohibitive ordinance would be welcome. (Figures 18 and 19.)

As already stated, the towns of Switzerland were not singular in enacting sumptuary legislation, for many other cities, especially in Germany, felt called upon to make such regulations. For comparison one may take Strassburg, not far down the Rhine, where the classification of the inhabitants and their garments was even more exhaustive than any so far quoted.

On April 2, 1660, the city council of that famous town passed an ordinance devoted almost entirely to costume or materials of dress, which is most meticulous in detail. Extracts from the introductory matter show the spirit of the government, which through its Burgermaster and Rath proclaimed the following intentions:

We have for many years observed with great governmental displeasure that not only all good ordinances alike are trodden under foot, that arrogance and pride without shame have been exhibited

Fig. 19.   Swiss Sunday Costumes.   Upper class, 17th Century.

by more and more from day to day, and finally, almost no difference between upper and lower ranks has been observed, but also the punishments have been with irresponsible opposition despised and thrown to the winds, and since we do not wish to draw down righteous divine vengeance and punishment upon us and the common people of the city we have examined, revised, and renewed the former clothing ordinance. [1629]

1.   We shall keep a watchful eye upon men and women, young and old, who wear improper, luxurious clothing and boldly despise our well-meant reminders.

2.   And among such improper, luxurious, trifling, indecent things,

contrary to old German ways will not unjustly be counted undue innovations in clothing. When either man or woman as soon as they see something new in clothing from foreign non-German nations, and imitate this regardless of whether it looks good or bad, and through such foolishness let it be seen how little they have the commendable steadfastness for which our old German forefathers had a

Fig. 20. Strassburg.
Young woman about 1650.

By Wenzel Hollar.

singular reputation in other things as well as in clothing, attention will be given at once. (Figure 20.)

Item. When men whose rank does not permit it go about the streets either without mantles, or wear mantles which are insufficient for their proper use.

Item. When persons who own no horse, or seldom mount another's, constantly jingle about in boots and spurs and shamelessly appear thus in the churches and before the altar taking the holy communion.

Item. When men ornament their hair like women, weave silk ribbons, ringlets, and other things in their wigs, and add other female fancies.

Item. When women and girls wear short, cut-off clothing which is shameful and vexatious.

Item. When they have neck-mantles on which the wide transparent ribbons expose the bosom, or are so small that they do not conceal the triffling mind.

Item. When they go about in high, wide, perforated shoes, stockings of uncommon luxurious colors, shoe-ribbons long, loose, and wide, or colored, with hanging garters.

Item. When women in summer time wear only light short aprons over their chemises and appear on the streets in such vexatious clothing.

Item. When married women with hair hanging in braids, or even in false hair, dare to appear before us the government, or in the churches, or in public gatherings like weddings, christenings, and dances.

Item. When women otherwise disfigure themselves improperly and luxuriously, wear uncommon colored clothing, allow themselves to be dressed in foreign and suspicious styles, or bring in a despicable and vexatious innovation in clothing and are displeasing to modest German and Christian souls, we shall give diligent attention to the matter.

The ordinance then divides the population into six classes, beginning at the bottom with a first rank which includes all maids, waitresses, seamstresses, and other single females who work for wages, whether or not their parents belong to a grade above the third. The second class is a male counterpart of the first, consisting of all men working for daily pay, and the list enumerates some twenty-nine occupations, from woodcutters on.

The third rank names first all kinds of handworkers, in a list of nearly one hundred trades then known in Strassburg. Also in the third class are "common citizens," bookkeepers, tradesmen owning property not over a thousand gulden in value, inferior musicians, schoolmasters without degrees, gardeners owning two or more horses, and others, up to a number of eighteen more occupations. Finally come city employees in lower positions, of whom at least twenty-seven kinds were operating.

Of the fourth class the lower grade included certain minor officials, notary candidates, musicians above playing for dances, clock-makers, various kinds of art-workers, printers who have their own plants, and other forms of business, of which all together about twenty-five kinds are enumerated. In the upper tier of the fourth rank were to be found more important city officials, including the postmaster and the

Fig. 21.   Strassburg.
Young woman about 1650.
By Wenzel Hollar.

master of the mint.   As to persons in various occupations whose qualifications for the fourth rank were in doubt, the decision was left to the police judge as to their proper place.

Merchants with fair to middle-sized business were placed in the lower rank of the fifth class, along with persons from the fourth class who had been elected sheriffs. Included also were candidates for the doctorate or licentiate far enough along to practice their professions. In the upper grade of this group were to be found the aristocracy of long residence, such as those families whose ancestors had been in government a hundred years back and who still carried themselves appropriately. Included also were men who lived on their own income, merchants from prominent families of the upper class who still conducted large enterprises, officials of the upper grades, with doctors, licentiates, and professors who have attained their academic degrees.

Fig. 22.   Strassburg.
Bride about 1650.
By Wenzel Hollar.

Last of all, the sixth class took in the actual government. Executives, members of the Great Council past and present, any noble subjects of the city, city attorneys, and such elevated officials as enjoyed the privileges of a superior group.

This long description is only the introduction to the law itself. In double the space given to these general principles and the definition of ranks, the law then took up each class and its subdivisions and prescribed the garments and ornaments which each group might or might not wear. Often a price was fixed which the wearer must not exceed, the amount expanding as one goes up the scale of classes.

With a wonderful intricacy of detail in describing costume or jewelry, the document not only paints the people as the law expected them to look, but reveals the circles in which they moved, the trades they followed, and the privileges of wealth exempt from labor.

IX. CLOTHING. EIGHTEENTH CENTURY

THE restrictions of the seventeenth century went forward with force into the next period, but they show changes of fashion which had to be suppressed or permitted. The ordinance of Bern of 1708 is characteristic of the time, and exhibits local features in contents and arrangement which call for brief attention.

After the usual complaint of neglect the law takes up certain dress materials which seem to be sources of extravagance and calls attention to the way in which these may or may not be used. Velvet and silk were first attacked, then gold and silver, then linen goods, and finally mourning garb, before the specific rules for the dress of men and women were laid down. All together some twenty-five duodecimo pages were devoted to these matters, in a document which is printed under the title " Ordinance against Pride and Superfluity in Clothing and also other Excesses and Luxuries." (*Ordnung wider den Pracht und Überfluss in Kleidern wie auch andere Excessen und Üppigkeiten.*) Many of the restrictions are familiar from earlier laws, but the exemptions show alterations in the tone of authorities in their contest with fashion, as well as an evident desire to preserve old Swiss habits and keep out foreign goods.

Everybody was forbidden without distinction of times or places to wear smooth and flowered velvet, satin, brocatel, brocard, or linen velvet of any color or form whatever. Nevertheless, exception was made for smooth and flowered velvet, satin, and damask on official caps (*Barette*), and facings on mantles, casaque sleeves, scarfs, and bonnets. Suits made entirely of damask, or vests of the same, should be worn only on Sundays or feast-days. Silk mantles remain as heretofore permitted, as well as the less costly silk goods, like taffeta, or anything which does not exceed that in price, and these materials could even be worn on week-days if they were used only for aprons, bosoms, camisoles, and the lining of mantles.

Men could wear silk vests on week-days, provided they do not go too far in price and expense, and conform to this ordinance on the wearing of silk. Children, boys or girls,

Fig. 23.   Germany.   Early Seventeenth Century.

must not have in any garment silk, satin, or plush, nor new scarlet and good cloth until they have completed their fifteenth year. They may wear in a modest way silk in their caps, and facings.

The restrictions on the use of gold and silver for dress ornament are similar to the rules in other places. Thread or fringes of this material on garments must not be used except on notable military or civic occasions, yet by a seeming contradiction articles of solid gold or silver were allowed. Enamel work, pearls, and precious stones must not be used except in rings already made, and here a reasonable moderation must be displayed. Observing that great sums have been wasted on wedding rings, it is ordered that only plain gold without settings shall be used.

The chapter on linen has a marked protective flavor, in that no cloth of this kind made outside of the Swiss Confederation can be used under penalty of a heavy fine, with exception of what may be needed for collars, scarfs, cuffs, hoods, and church headdresses. Foreign laces of silk or thread were forbidden because unnecessary, and serve only pride, while they draw much money out of the country. Nor shall there be employed in the place of these any costly adornments of fine cloth or linen, except; — and here the authorities show again their fine appreciation of the details of apparel, — except that men may have about their necks for the protection of their coat collars a very small band of lace which must not display either excess or expensiveness, and lace also may be used on the hoods of young children, provided that it is neither more costly, nor larger, nor wider than already prescribed. No one else may use these foreign products. Twisted silk fringes on gloves (*händschen*) or elsewhere must not be worn, and disobedience to any of these provisions was subject to a graduated fine for the first, second, and third offense.

The wearing of mourning for relatives was fixed according to lines used in other places already considered here. The council, however, protested against the excesses of common custom and cited the oft-recurring cases where a father or mother on the death of a little child of minor age have furnished seven, eight, or more persons with an entire outfit of mourning clothing. This great expense was reduced by ordering that only the parents and children of the family should wear full mourning, and others the *petit deuil*. Mourning clothing in general must be moderate, with the further understanding that the mourning mantle should be no longer than the ordinary garment, and the crape on men regulated by that pattern, while the crape for women should reach only to the knee.

Further particulars respecting the dress of men, women, and servants occupy some twelve pages more of this ordi-

Fig. 24.   Germany.   Seventeenth Century.

nance and deserve attention for their local color. As in other places, wigs were a source of irritation to the authorities, and it was ordered that no one under twenty years of age might wear this adornment except in cases of necessity, which were to be allowed at the discretion of the Chamber of Reform. Other civilian citizens could have wigs, provided they were worn with moderation, but totally forbidden were all such as stood high over the forehead, or the annoying long, knotted pigtail wigs, or any other display of disgraceful expense, including the excessive use of powder.

Clergy and students who wear this artificial hair must, in order to distinguish them from civilians, have only small round wigs which reach to the coat collar and no farther, and these must not be raised up over the forehead. These classes must also as heretofore avoid silk waistcoats, silk coat collars, costly linen, and too wide collars, and in general must set a good example.

As to women, the authorities clearly recognized a change in fashions, for the first thing ordered was that in future the so-called *Bernoise* made of gauze, a form of bonnet, may be permitted. Also the *Angloise*, with the restraint that upon this and the *Bernoise* only a single band of folded ribbon without gold or silver may be worn. Maidservants may not have either of these articles, even if they have received them as gifts.

The offensive short aprons, or *menageres*, are forbidden, but the large lace cuffs called *Engageantes* may be worn by anyone who so desires, provided they do so in moderation. Black scarfs remain permitted, but must be made only of taffeta without any ribbons or lace. On the other hand, women must cease to wear not only the excessively large *Steinkerques*, *Mouchoirs*, or neckcloths, whatever the form, and especially the recently introduced *Tours*, *Palatines*, or neckwear made of sable, ermine, or other costly foreign furs, or, in fact, any other expensive furs.

The so-called mantles remained in favor, and could be worn in church, but they must be made in accordance with materials allowed on different days of the week. These mantles, as well as the German dress, must not trail on the ground, and only one petticoat of silk at a time could be worn by anyone. Particularly forbidden were the unseemly figured silk garments, the so-called *furies*.

The authorities intended that in future all clothing should be worn plain and smooth, and especially on over and under-garments there should be no fringes, laces, crape or similar trimmings, and in particular none of the new-fashioned apron flounces (*Falbalas*). It was to be understood, however, that the words "plain" and "smooth" do not exclude the ribbon which may be set on the edge of the skirt, provided this is plain.

Fig. 25. Germany. About 1630.

Feathered scarfs were allowed if made from native ducks or skins, but when made of ostrich feathers and the like, or having fringes, lace, sable, or other costly foreign fur, they were totally forbidden, along with any ribbons attached. At communion service all well-to-do women and girls must appear in black. Women of the clergy should set a good example in moderation but will be fined for excesses in dress just the same.

Neither men nor women could have shoes made outside of Bern territory, nor be allowed to have them sent in from outside, nor to buy foreign shoes in the market. Shoes and slippers must in future be manufactured of no other material than leather, felt, or cloth and people were forbidden to have lace, cords, ribbons, or other trimming, except what is necessary for cloth shoes, and must be without any embroidery, needle work, or ornamentation whatever.

Young children must be clothed according to this ordinance and all excess of ribbons and feathers on their hats and caps avoided. They should be taught from their youth up modesty, discipline, and honor, otherwise all excess will be punished according to the case. Children were allowed to wear black or white taffeta, gauze, or crape, and the so-called *negliges*, provided they were not made of forbidden material.

Servants should retain as long as they can the costume which they brought from the country into the city. Neither manservant nor maid may wear a silk neckcloth, or ragged scarf, or anything else of the kind, except a simple ironed (*gebrättelte*) collar, and they must be clothed in native cloth, cheap woolen or similar smooth material. Those maids who were permitted to wear caps could have only skunk skin or other cheap fur, without velvet bottom, or they might have hoods, caps, and the like, made of cloth and entirely smooth. All other caps, including such as may have been gifts from their mistresses; all forms of lace on the hoods except the small permitted peasant lace; all gold headdresses at christenings, because these are not fitting adornments; and in general all costliness and superfluity were forbidden. Even shoes for man or maid must be either black or oiled.[1]

After all these " don'ts " in regard to wearing apparel we

---

[1] The frequent use of French words in the ordinances of Bern points to two conditions in that canton. First, that a large portion of the population spoke that language and naturally used dress terms of their own which were often seen in ordinances in their own tongue. Second, that this circumstance made it easier for fashions from France to invade that region.

may stop for a moment to consider a description of people as they actually appeared in the eighteenth century, written by a Swiss author [2] of great learning and antiquarian zeal. Such an account covers a longer period than it would in these days, for changes in fashion took place more slowly.

Fig. 26.   Germany.   Seventeenth Century.

At that time civic authorities were much concerned over the introduction of new foreign styles, but they governed a conservative people, and encountered no revolutions in clothing such as the twentieth century has witnessed.

In those days men wore a coat reaching below the waist, made without a collar and decorated with buttons. The sleeves were short and wide, with broad facings out of which

[2] Finsler, *Zurich im achtzehnten Jahrhundert*, 196, etc.

projected cuffs reaching to the wrists. For festive occasions these cuffs were decorated with lace. The back of the coat was made with several folds which caused it to stand out stiff, and under this was a long vest which reached almost to

Fig. 27. Germany. Seventeenth Century.

the knee. Both coat and vest had pockets closed with flaps which were adorned with lace and buttons so richly embroidered that on pleasure walks or visits the coat was left open for general display. The short trousers were bound under the knee, but not with special garters as in former days.

Around the neck was worn a rather long scarf with the lower ends sometimes drawn through button-holes. Stockings were either white or black, and when worn on Sundays or festal occasions were often made of silk. For footwear, boots were used only for riding, while shoes began to have

Fig. 28.   Germany.   Seventeenth Century.

a modern look, although often tied with silver strings, while the clergy denied themselves this latter extravagance. The heavily powdered wig was already in fashion, and along with this the men whitened their natural hair, but gradually the queue and the hair-bag came into use, and some of the artificiality disappeared. The small three-cornered hat was commonly carried under the arm, evidently for reasons of style rather than health, and the hands were well occupied,

for no man went out without his sword and cane, the latter
attached to his hand by a ribbon.

Members of the small and large councils were usually
clothed in black, over which they wore a black mantle, similar to that of the clergy, but without sleeves. On civil and
religious holidays they wore ruffs thick with countless folds
about the neck and on the head a barette, though on ordinary
Sundays a smooth neck-band (*Beſſschen*) and a small hat

Fig. 29.　Swiss Men's Costumes.　18th Century.

a. Magistrate.　b. and c. Citizens.

were sufficient. This mantle and neck-band formed also the
church dress, *bürgerliche Tracht*, for other citizens for public
occasions and funerals, while at the same time colored clothing might be worn underneath. Theological candidates must
dress in black and wear in classes or disputations a modest
ruff, while other students, including the younger scholars,
must have the black mantle with smooth collars. The academic robe is still with us, bearing a long history both before
and after the eighteenth century. (Figure 29.)

The women's dress considered proper for both house and
street consisted of skirt and waist sewn together to form the

Nachtrok. A literal translation of that word would be misleading, for it was neither a night robe nor an evening dress, but a conventional term for what we should probably call a street dress. Permissible for the house while performing household duties, the *Schöpen* was a loose garment or gown with flaps attached. Dress sleeves were narrow at the top, becoming wider at the elbow, where they were ornamented with borders, either wide or narrow, while the forearm was covered with broad white shirt sleeves, which were sometimes short leaving the arm free, sometimes ending in cuffs. Hoop-skirts were much in favor, and sometimes overran the size allowed by ordinances. Aprons were long and wide, and were worn in public when on visits or while taking pleasure walks. Around the neck women wore a ribbon or a band of up-standing muslin, a neck-scarf brought forward, a neck chain, or on the breast a ribbon or something of the sort.

Powdered hair was usual for women whether married, single, or young girls. On the head rested a small flat hat ornamented with plain stripes or simple lace, while on the left side of the forehead a small bouquet of artificial flowers, a cluster of pearls, or some similar ornament might be fastened. Toquets, feathers, flowers were forbidden by law, but prominent women began to wear them and we may assume that the fashion spread. In winter all kinds of warm hoods were in use and the *Kaputze* or monk's hood might have been seen with a street dress.

Women's church dress must be sober black as it had been for centuries, but changes in costume were visible. Up to 1755 the prescribed headdress for church was the *Tüchli*, the white covering like the nun's hood, but afterward substitutes began to be permitted and this form gradually went out of use. Thereafter the law required that the headdress and neck-scarf should be made of black gauze or taffeta, and plain without lace or fringes. The dress itself must be of smooth black burat with apron of the same material.

Brides and single women sponsors at christenings belonging to the burger class continued to wear the *Schäppeli*. This was a rather high, richly decorated crown or hat of cylindrical form, fitting so closely to the head that the top hair could not be seen, while two long braids hung down the back. On such occasions a rich girdle, gold chains on the neck and breast, and even gold bracelets might be worn. In winter both men and women carried muffs, which were attached to the body by a girdle, often of an expensive character. (Figure 30.)

This description of costume in Zurich will serve also as a

Fig. 30.   Swiss Women's Costumes.   18th Century.

    a. Church dress with *Tüchli*.
    b. With hat like a fire-bucket.
    c. With *Rosenkappe*.

picture of dress in Basel and Bern with minor variations in detail. In all of these cities the laws against excess were continued or repeatedly reënacted to the close of the century, and it remains to be seen what new difficulties or new fashions were encountered by the makers of ordinances. The question of enforcement is a matter which will be taken up in a later chapter.

The ordinances continue to the close of the eighteenth century to forbid the use of many articles of dress and ornament which earlier governments had made unlawful. Jewels, pearls, precious stones, gold and silver filagree work were prohibited, except that some of them might be used for finger rings, ear ornaments, or the decoration of hoods. Velvet must not be used for outer garments but only for linings. Furs like sable, ermine, or marten were closely restricted. Laces made of silk, unless they were black, might not be worn, unless permitted by exceptions which were sometimes based upon cost and sometimes on the rank of the wearer. Satin and damask had restrictions for the upper classes, and the lower orders might not have them at all. Not always alike in the wording of their laws, the three cities all attempted to stop the expenditure of money on costly personal decoration.

The contest over costume in general lay between the conservative sentiment of the authorities and the new fashions which they saw creeping in over the borders. The law required that the Reformation-Chamber should be made up of men of mature age, and they were actually chosen from prominent and even eminent citizens. Their rules and decisions seem out of place in the twentieth century, but we are obliged to give them serious consideration in the light of the period. At the same time we shall have to inquire why they were obliged to pass new sumptuary ordinances every few years, even in the eighteenth century. In each of these cities during some ninety years before the French Revolution more than twenty such laws were enacted or repeated at the average rate of one about every four years. (Figure 31.)

In spite of the repetitions, there are a few matters which require our attention in this legislation before looking into its effectiveness or the manner of its execution. During a century costume itself underwent certain modifications. At the end of the period citizens wore plain collars instead of ruffs, and it will be worth while to see if the lawmakers have been moved by changes of mode.

Keeping in mind the numerous restrictions on the display of jewelry and the use of laces and dress materials which continued to the end of the century, the rules endeavor to maintain differences in rank, and go into details of costume which invoke our admiration for the observing powers of the authorities. In Basel in 1715 the class distinctions were strongly reiterated, and officials and citizens were admonished to appear in public in their proper clothing. Women were earnestly forbidden to wear the shamefully short garments, the wide openings at the neck, or display the trifling

Fig. 31. Basel. Old and new fashions
in 18th Century.

exposure which may be expected of prostitutes and people of that kind when brought before the Court of Marital Relations (*Ehegericht*).

Compared to this ordinance of eighteen quarto pages, the law of 1727 covers but eleven, and instead of eleven pages devoted to sumptuary regulation there are two and one-half, a contrast which continues through most of the ordinances of the eighteenth century. At the same time the councils kept a watchful eye upon innovations. Wedding costs were to be checked by ruling that the gifts between groom and bride must not exceed three hundred *thaler* and the cost of the ring was limited to two hundred. *Volanten*, or *fliegende Nachtrok*, a loose dress with long flaps, must not be seen on

Fig. 32. Germany. Seventeenth Century.

the street, and a fine was threatened for any one who introduced a new fashion; yet the law against *volanten* does not seem to have been completely effective, for they are forbidden again in 1742 for street or even carriage wear.

In 1750 the street dress might be made of wool, cotton, or linen without embroidery, but in 1780 might be made of silk, though not of muslin, velvet, or similar heavy goods, and without trimmings or any linings of sable or costly fur. As to mantillas, only black color was allowed, and in church must be worn closed. If made of fur there must be no edging attached, and a fine was again set on the introduction of new fashions because "we look upon it as one of the greatest evils." Feathers must not be worn except on sleigh-rides, nor anything in place of them made of wood, straw, thorns, or whatever it may be. Veils must not be worn in church, nor hoop-skirts anywhere unless with a complete Basel costume.

In Zurich and elsewhere at the beginning of the eighteenth century, a bonnet or hood was in style which covered the sides of the head and projected forward and downward in a point. In 1702 it was enacted that this point should not come down farther than the middle of the forehead. About the same time there was a large hat called a "Ship" which rested on top of the head, and whose broad rim curved gently downward like the deck of a boat bottom-side up. This phenomenon does not seem to appear in the laws, but an ordinance of Bern in 1703 speaks with indignant clearness on female fashion when it outlaws the "vexatious short aprons, the so-called *menageres*," as well as the "ugly *engageantes*, the long lace cuffs hanging downward." (Figures 33 and 34.)

As the century advanced regulations were frequently issued with contents similar to those already considered, but it was evident that new things had come up for restriction. For instance, books appear bound in tortoise-shell or decorated with solid gold mountings. These were evidently prayer-books or hymnals, but the council of Zurich said in 1744 that these must not be used. Watches were now carried, but women must not have any made of silver, nor is anyone permitted to have one of solid gold, nor should they have solid tobacco boxes or sword mountings in that metal. Swiss-made lace not over an inch wide might be used on women's caps, but with their eternal vigilance the authorities forbade the exposure of shoulders and ordered collars to be

closed. As to the pocket time-piece, a contest with fashion
may be seen in the ordinance of 1779 and repeated in 1790,
where it was forbidden to carry *more than one* watch, and
the chain must have no other pendants than a key, a seal.
and a hook or clasp.

The regulation of children's clothing was not a new duty
of the city council, but the special ordinance of 1778 in
Zurich explained the lawful costume of the rising generation
for the remainder of the century. The council observed with

Fig. 33.   Swiss Costume about 1650–1660.

regret that there was a growing extravagance in the clothing
of youth, and they met this with a statement of rules. Under
these orders children of both sexes must have no trimmings
of any kind on their clothing, nor use any kind of fur except
for muffs and gloves. They were forbidden to wear watches
and all jewelry except such earrings of any metal they might
choose, while shoe buckles and such like must be made only
of plain silver or some simple metal. Up to their eighth year
they could have their hair dressed, but must use only their
own hair. Along with this coiffure nothing but a toupet,
chignon, and on either side a buckle could be worn. Boys'

clothing was restricted to wool, linen, and cotton, with exception of cotton velvet. Girls were permitted to wear silk dresses as hitherto, but after their fifteenth year they must conform to the general ordinances for women's clothing and headdresses. All of these regulations were practically the same in the law of 1790.

The history of the hoop-skirt covers more than two centuries of this period, and had its ins and outs in fashionable esteem. Switzerland was in this current like the rest, although

Fig. 34. Basel. About 1700.
The " Ship " Hat.

the use of this article was confined by law to the better classes and forbidden to servants and the lower orders. Objections to this feature continued to the end, and whatever may have been the sentiments of the women, the law still said in 1790 that crinoline must not be worn in Zurich.

Small relaxations in the details of the ordinances are seen from time to time, as the authorities reluctantly permit modifications of garments previously forbidden, and the fines for disobedience change with the temper of the councils. The general form of costume remained about the same during the century, but the ornamentation of the person and the clothing underwent changes, which authorities did not fail to observe and restrict or reprimand. The sumptuary laws as a whole were less voluminous than many enacted in the seventeenth century, and sometimes the later rules counselled moderation instead of ordering proscription, but the intention to curb expense was never wanting. To appreciate the

Fig. 35.   Germany.   Seventeenth Century.

legislative power left in the hands of these city governments, we must contemplate not only the regulation of personal expenditure but the multitude of laws, both local and international, which issued from their chambers. How far they obtained obedience to their sumptuary rules is another matter.

From one item in the act of 1744 it would appear that tobacco boxes might be allowed if they were not made of

solid gold, and we may consider for a moment the story of
that plant in Switzerland. Its use met with resistance everywhere, and in the various cantons the seventeenth century
witnessed the enactment of prohibitory ordinances, in which
two motives stand out prominently. One was the danger to
health and the other the risk of fire from smoking, though

Fig. 36.   Germany.   Seventeenth Century.

in neither case was the cost of the habit conspicuously in
mind.

Not going back too far we find an ordinance of Bern in
1659 which prohibited tobacco, and a similar law in 1661,
while in 1675 the use was forbidden because it was regarded
as a form of suicide. Any traveler found with tobacco in his
possession was to have a humiliating punishment in the work
house or exposure in the cage (*Schellenwerk oder Trille*).

In 1684 and again in 1689 dealers were placed under the ban of the law, and at intervals the ordinances against the use of the weed were renewed and carried over into the eighteenth century. In 1710 smoking and snuff-taking were still subject to fines, but by 1719 the planting of tobacco had been brought into the country, and the era of laws about its culture and against smuggling soon began.

In Zurich the council passed another law on July 13, 1671, forbidding the sale of this article, but on October 23 received a petition from local dealers in protest, on the ground that the sale was free outside the city territory and their business was injured. The reply of the government was firm and unequivocal. All steps must be taken to stop this pernicious habit. Dealers may sell to strangers but not to Zurich citizens. Smoking in gilds, assemblies, and other places is absolutely forbidden, for " this deleterious kraut must be stamped out."

In 1686 two merchants refused to pay a fine of twenty-five pounds because the sale of tobacco was a common custom and they were the first to be punished. Apparently the dealers were standing together to get a repeal of the law, but in vain, for we find in 1691 that smoking, chewing, and taking snuff are all forbidden, and in 1697 the council decreed that all previous ordinances were to stand, with no smoking on the streets.

The ordinances of the eighteenth century continue to restrict the use of tobacco to the end of the period, but they take on the aspect of fire risk rather than restraint of bad habits. The prevention of fire can be readily understood in cities where many wooden buildings still existed, in spite of the changes to stone and brick after the earthquakes and conflagrations of other days. Arrests for smoking did occur, but at long intervals, and we are not always sure whether they were for bad habits or bad situations. The records of the Reformation-Chamber of Zurich show periods of a dozen years where no one was brought up for this misdemeanor, and the shorter intervals leave the number very small. The gold snuff-box was recognized in the law, and the habits of the people governed the extent of prosecutions.

X. JOURNEYS TO BADEN (*BADENFAHREN*)

ZURICH had a problem which does not appear in the ordinances of the other cities. This was the habit of making trips to a nearby watering-place, where the ordinary frugality of the citizen was likely to meet defeat in the search for refreshment and health. This resort was Baden, situated in the canyon of Argau, where mineral springs furnished the medical reasons, and the distance from Zurich was only fourteen miles. For three centuries of our period these springs attracted visitors, and during nearly the whole of that time the custom is visible in the laws. The points of attack were the expense of this journey and the relaxation of steady habits in the social whirl which there prevailed.

When prominent persons of Zurich made this journey it was known in advance, and friends gathered together with gifts and perhaps accompanied them part of the way out in a festal procession. This was not a farewell salutation, for everybody knew they were coming back, but an occasion for congratulations, like a birthday or a wedding anniversary The journey on horseback or in carriage probably consumed half a day, but when you were there you supposed you were free from the restraints of the home town, and might eat what you pleased, adorn yourself with the fine garments which the Zurich law forbade, and enjoy to the full the whirl of society.

Trouble began at an early date. In 1529 the trip was forbidden because the dead were left unburied and the sick made to take Roman Catholic sacrament, and second, because there was too much extravagance. Feasting and gambling in private houses instead of in public taverns was met with another fine, yet that same year the authorities relented somewhat and said the journey might be made, but parting gifts must cease, and only a modest remembrance might be offered on the return.

A hundred years later the fashion still remained, and in

1628 the law said there should be no gifts of gold, silver, or live sheep, either on going or returning. Close relatives might send a modest meal, but all other honors were forbidden. This rule was repeated in 1636, with the remark that excessive expense had been going on in recent years, much to the cost of the givers and of no particular use to the receivers. In 1650 Baden trips on Sunday must wait till after preaching, and on that day there must be no procession of friends, no gifts, nor celebration. Nine years later the excursion was again totally forbidden, but by 1671 the court reported that Baden gifts were a returning evil and recommended that restraint be placed on the use of Saturday or Sunday for such trips. But the evil continued, with attempts at restriction without much result, for in 1685 a man was arraigned for receiving a Baden gift from a gild, and he objected to a fine because he was the first to be arrested since the ordinance of 1680.

Saturday as a time for starting was forbidden in 1691 and again in 1697, and if you must go on Sunday just " for a change of air " you must have the permit of the president of the Reformation-Chamber. Excessive cost of clothing and outfit for honor processions was again put under restraint, and gifts at going or returning forbidden under threat of a heavy fine and confiscation. For some time such gifts to officials going to their posts in the country had likewise been unlawful, but the custom was hard to overcome. In 1755 the authorities noted that Baden gifts were coming into use again and imposed a fine, while they made it clear that the rules of Zurich regarding dress and luxury would be applied to citizens while in Baden as well as when at home.

By 1770 it is said that such purely watering-place ceremonies went out of use, but it must be noted that another custom had gradually come into its place. Officials civil, or clerical, on the way to their positions might be accorded such honors, but the ordinances fix a low limit for each grade of office, so that a deputy-governor might be accompanied by only four gentlemen, a low official by one, with a fine for any excess display of this kind. As we come to the end of this story the prohibitions are still in the law. In 1785 all gifts, either from communities or persons to officials, whether in silver-ware or money value, were again forbidden under penalty of fine and confiscation.

Fig. 37   Germany.   Seventeenth Century.

This century-long attempt to regulate a popular impulse is quite in line with conception of government at the time, and we have to look carefully into the cost of such occasions. Receiving the honor was only one part of the display, for the recipient was expected to be generous in entertainment in return. If the law could regulate the clothing and banquets of private citizens it could certainly restrain the cost of these public occasions.

XI. SLEIGHRIDING

SLEIGHRIDING was another subject which seemed to demand attention in these cities. Ordinances on this point do not appear early in the period, and the motives form a combination of moral, sumptuary, and ordinary police reasoning, with varying weight laid upon these factors. The irregularity of its appearance in the courts tempts one to guess at the state of the weather, or the severity of the winters, since the snowfall in that climate is by no means uniform. Yet sledding had a long history in Switzerland, whether or not it appears in the laws.

In Zurich in 1663 the Reformations-Kammer suggested to the council that sleighriding be forbidden, as it led to a waste of time and was the cause of much frivolity. In 1669 an ordinance prescribed that it must not be indulged in after *Bätzyt* (night bell), while in 1691 a law against night disturbances included sleighriding, not only inside but also outside the fortifications, because it was not only a great expense but a serious annoyance. The same prohibition was decreed in 1697, but the fine reduced from fifty pounds to twenty.

In Bern in 1667 it was unlawful to ride in a sleigh on Sunday, but in 1708 a moral and social reason was given for the restraint of this practice. Complaint was entered that great danger to young people was incurred by allowing boys and girls to ride together late at night. Such practice was unbecoming to women even in daytime, therefore the sex was forbidden to sleighride except when a man took his wife or children out to his farm or into the country. When men went out they must take their sleighs off the street at nightfall or be fined twenty pounds. Parents were made liable for the fines of children living at home, and those separated or without parents must pay their own penalties.

It is evident that sleighing parties were not content with

the mere motion of the vehicle, for an ordinance of Basel in 1742 decreed that dancing must stop at midnight, and the expense of refreshments must not exceed one and a half gulden per person, not including wine and musicians, rules which remained in the law for a dozen years or more. Zurich said in 1755 that the driving of sleighs would be permitted for business uses only, but later for a quarter of a century it appeared to be a matter of expense so far as new laws were concerned, for it was ordered that coaches and sleighs when permitted were to be plainly painted and trimmed with cloth or plush, with no gilding or carving and no gold ornaments on the harness. During the eighteenth century Zurich was fairly diligent in the prosecutions of cases under the sleigh law. The record of the Reformations-Kammer shows that one or another of the aspects of the ordinances was in effect, for during the twenty-seven years in which the matter came before the court some four hundred and seventeen cases were adjudged, ranging all the way from two to seventy-seven per year. But we have also to consider that forty-six years of that period passed without any record of arrest for this misdemeanor, and the diligence of the authorities is open to question.

AS already indicated, the enforcement of sumptuary regulations and minor police laws was placed under secular supervision in Basel and Zurich at the time of the religious Reformation in Switzerland, while Bern, although Protestant, continued in authority the *Chorgericht*, or consistory, until late in the seventeenth century. The records of these courts in Bern and Zurich have in the course of time suffered much loss, but in Basel the docket of the Reformations-Kammer is continuous for a period of one hundred and twenty-two years, from 1674 to 1796. Selections from this record showing years of special activity indicate how far the government of Basel went in the execution of its own sumptuary ordinances.

In 1681, for example, the Reformation-Chamber met on Wednesdays thirty-eight times during the year, and the minutes cover some thirty-eight pages of medium size. In January, February, and March of that year the cases were mostly due to non-observance of Sunday laws, either for walking out the gates or for teaming at forbidden hours. Others were for the mild offense of leaving the cathedral by a forbidden door, or concerned an open quarrel over a pew. The ordinary police powers of the court were displayed in the case of Ludwig Keller, one of the court employees, who was charged with going home " *voll und toll,*" the offense being further aggravated by cursing. His excuse was that his wife never gave him a good word. She was in fact a papistical woman, and often wished to throw him out by force. The reply was not considered sufficient, and Ludwig was ordered to spend one night in the gate-house. It seems that he also had a quarrel with Jacob Thomas, the bell-ringer, for calling him a drunkard, but Jacob said he had used these harsh but accurate terms while attempting to collect a debt.

April began with police cases, but was soon busy with dress delinquencies. Maria Ritter was asked why in the face

101

of the published mandate she appeared in the meat market in her loose underdress. She pleaded ignorance. She was indeed without her girdle, but had not thought its absence meant so much, yet it seemed to mean something to eighteen other women, mostly servants, who were called up the same day for that offense.

Margaret, a servant, was seen wearing marten fur and double lace trimmings, but the dress turned out to be a gift from her mistress and she was dismissed with a warning. J. Mottler had a very long wig and was fined, but Hans Schneider was given a chance to let his hair grow again. Sara Grumm, Burgermeister Burckhardt's maid, was out on the street in her underdress because a gentleman was sick in the house and she had to run to the apothecary shop in such haste that she could not put on her breastpiece. But the court was hard-hearted and imposed a fine. .

Summer seemed to be arriving, for in April and May twelve other women were cited for their bare necks. A jacket seen in the market place worn by a lady living nearby who thought she could go that far without trouble was met only by a fine. One excused herself this error because she had a swelling on her breast, another because she had bad breath and was pregnant, while others pleaded ignorance of the law or short distances in vain, but a widow in poverty who wore the only old bosom she possessed was leniently dismissed.

Elizabeth Mender said she had a sick mother and was obliged to watch the dye-kettle herself. This boiled up, and she was compelled in haste to run out in her house dress to get the color-stuff, but she was fined just the same. Accused of keeping a negligent household, cursing, swearing, desecration of the Sabbath and neglect of church, a certain J. B. answered that he went to church regularly, and as to swearing at his wife he was probably cited because he came home late one night after spending an evening with a friend, and his wife talked rather loud. He was ordered to spend the night in the water tower, but a week later he appeared in behalf of his wife, who was melancholy and hysterical, and would run away rather than come into court. She admitted cursing and swearing and promised to do better. She was informed that she ought to appear in person, but it is not recorded that she did.

Mrs. Elizabeth Berb explained that her going about with bare bosom occurred near her home. In fact, she had put

Fig. 38.   Germany.   Eighteenth Century.

everything she had in the cellar for a fortnight and could not find the breastpiece. Anna Wurz said that her wearing her house dress on the street was because she was taken out unexpectedly by a brother into one of the suburbs and did not notice the absence of her bosom cover.

The work of the Reformation-Chamber is perhaps sufficiently indicated by these varied examples taken from the docket of 1681. The court, or perhaps informers, were very busy during the year, the nature of offenses changing somewhat with the season. One month the cases largely concerned costume, and during another period Sunday excursions out of the city gates came to the front. It is evident that the loose house dress, *unterrock*, was the chief object of pursuit. The attempted repression of this garment cannot be classed as sumptuary in the sense of restraining expense. It was in the interest of morals, as then understood, that the law restrained the exposure of the person, and it promoted good form in the same way that insistence on the wearing of mantles or ruffs gave propriety or dignity in public places. Limitation of expense was sought in the rules about furs, ribbons, and laces on women, or wigs and scarfs on men.

The statistics of the activity of the court in 1681 are significant. Of 289 cases 133 persons were cited for unlawful clothing. Out of this 133 there were eighty-six presented for house dress, lack of lacing, or exposed arms on the street. Sixteen others wore their jackets without proper overgarment; and twenty-seven more, mostly servants, had to answer for fur, laces, or ribbons. Only seven men were called up for dress, and four of these wore excessively large wigs.

Other offenses included eighty-four persons for going outside the city gates at the wrong time on Sunday, eleven for other Sabbath troubles, while thirty were held for dancing and ten for profanity. The seventy-six cases dismissed leave more than one hundred convictions, making the number of persons presented for costume nearly equal to the total of all the rest.

The year 1682 showed a serious falling off in prosecutions. The offending garments were the same, but only forty-five women and three men were summoned to court for such troubles. The efforts of the watchers were evidently spent on persons who went outside the gates on Sunday, of whom sixty-six were called in, and some thirty others for drinking or selling on that day. Five for profanity and six for dancing filled up a total which showed a serious decline in zeal or an important reformation in manners since the last year, as you please.

The court met twenty-five times during the year 1682, and the variety of delinquencies was about the same as in 1681.

Fig. 39. Germany. Eighteenth Century.

A few cases and pronouncements are of interest. On Wednesday, May 3, 1682, at the regular meeting, Caspar Meyer was brought to the bar for coming to church in a neck-cloth instead of the regulation ruff. He answered that on the previous day he had had a tailor in his house, who inadvertently took away the key to the place where his neckwear was kept. That very night there came a heavy earthquake, and in view of this mighty manifestation of Providence he thought it would not do to miss church simply for the lack of a proper collar. Hence the " *Halstuch.*" He was excused. Later in the month the court expressed its displeasure with its watchers, declaring that they reported the delinquencies of serving maids and failed to see those of higher rank. The record of cases later on shows that this evil was not easily eradicated. One of the middle class appears to have been Johann Blechnagel's wife, who wore a costume which the court does not describe with exactness. Her dress seems to have been a failure in ensemble, or perhaps a lack of upper covering caused an accusation of " not being properly clad behind and before " (*Welche hinden und vornen nicht geziemend angethan gewesen*).

In 1685 the city council, in view of the increasing cost of domestic help, passed an ordinance which fixed the wages of such servants, expressing at the same time its regret that young housekeepers were exceeding the limits of such payments established by ordinances more than forty years before. Our regrets are less when we observe how much of her income a maid must sacrifice when she puts on clothing above her class or in some way against the law. The renewed ordinance says that a maid who does the whole housework is entitled to nine pounds per half year, with one-half a *reichstaler* as bargain money. A girl who does the kitchen work and milks the cows should get eight pounds, while a nursemaid can earn from four to six pounds in the same period. Any woman who pays more than these prices for such services is subject to a fine of two marks silver. In view of the changing values of money it is difficult to translate these wages into modern currency, but for the moment one may note that when a lady pays a fine of ten pounds for an illegal dress she is losing more cash than her housekeeper should earn in six months.

The last fifteen years of the seventeenth century furnish little new from Basel on the regulation of costume, due in part to neglect and in part to local conditions. In 1691 a political revolution stopped the work of the Reformation-

Chamber, and it met but once during the year. A revolt of the middle classes under Fatio and others made trouble for the authorities, but this was eventually suppressed with promises soon broken, and the aristocratic government was revived. The Grand Council ordered the Reformation to meet every week whether there was any business on hand or not, but that court met only once in December. By the following March the war on clothing began again.

The court in 1685 observed in a small way the march of fashion, and petitioned the council for a moderation of the rule requiring women to come to church in veils, suggesting that this point be omitted from the rules for the morning service, or left to the discretion of the Reformation-Chamber. This body seemed to be in a lenient mood that year, for when several women were cited in April for bare bosoms, and another wore a hood in church instead of her "*tüchli*," and two men had on neck-cloths instead of ruffs the whole lot were excused with admonitions only. On May 29 there was issued a long exhortation to better observance of the ordinance, but the secretary was tired and gave vent to his feelings in the minutes: "*Gott geb wie lang.*"

> "*Dem Screiber die Mühe, dem Trucker das Gelt,*
> *Zu wünchen das dess nicht spotten die Welt.*"

In Bern during the last quarter of the seventeenth century a reorganized Reformation-Chamber was in operation in the place of the Consistory noted earlier. Activity began in earnest in 1676 and continued until 1696, except that for a period of eight years between 1683 and 1692 the record is lost and the proceedings uncertain. However, the surviving docket can be studied to advantage while making comparisons with actions of the other Swiss cities.

The city council in a resolution of April 20, 1676, acknowledged its own share of blame for the increase of luxury and expense among the citizenry and held everyone of its own members to obedience to the ordinance for himself and for his family. The mandate of 1672 must be enforced in full, and any relaxation on the subject of sleeves formerly allowed was now rescinded.

The Reformation-Chamber voted to meet every Thursday, and began operations on May 25 with Herr Venner Kilchberger in the chair and six other prominent citizens completing the court. Eighteen sessions were held during the remainder of 1676, and eighty women and sixteen men had to answer for their garments. As might be expected, nearly all of these women were cited for short sleeves. Some were held for laces and others for wearing colored dresses in church instead of the prescribed attire, while all of the men sinned in long hair or wigs.

During the next few years both the number of sessions and the prosecutions for sumptuary disobedience fell off, but in 1682, with only twelve sessions, the citations for dress came back in force. Ninety-four women and twenty-five men had to answer at the bar. Women's sleeves were attracting less attention from the court, while other portions of apparel were made subjects of judicial scrutiny, as may be seen from a few selections from the docket.

Fräulein von Muller appeared in a dress which was built " wholly improper behind and before." One maid was reprimanded for her silk kerchief, and another was chided about cuffs and neck-pieces. Objectionable objects on women were gold and silver lace work, feathers in their bonnets, and coats that were made too long. Frau Captain Erlach was informed that she must wear her cap headdress a little smaller, while a young man with lace on his cravat had gone to church without a mantle and carried a cane. Ludwig Meij, Esquire, went out with gold buttons on his cloak, and other men were obliged to account for their long hair or their silver garters.

The loss of the records of the court for eight years is unfortunate, but during that interval something must have happened, for by 1692 the Reformation-Chamber came into action with more than usual vigor. Out of 260 cases noted for that year 163 were women and sixty-seven were men, and the following year was still worse, for 219 women and ninety-three men had to explain their dress.

In the trials in 1692 the accusations show a wide observation of costume, for the asserted delinquencies ranged from head to foot. Women were brought in for wearing mourning crepe of excessive length, and a servant maid was directed to make her cloak shorter. Two others of that class were conspicuous in red stockings, aggravated in one case by lace on her collar and a black silk scarf. A young lady was called in for appearing in a bonnet with tall gauze trimmings and

Fig. 40.   Germany.   Eighteenth Century.

for exposing her neck and bosom, upon which hung a gold chain and jewel. She was given time for reflexion and a diminished fine of ten pounds. She was matched by another young woman who was found walking about at night with boys, displaying a neckband made too broad with lace, her bare neck adorned with a gold necklace and her hair standing high under her bonnet.

The flat bonnet known as the *Bernoise* gave a great deal

of trouble. At one session in May all of twelve women were held for wearing this feature too high, and before the year closed the difficulty had become so great that the board passed a resolution that the new *Bernoises* might be worn but not by maidservants. Furthermore, the bonnet with its decoration must be only three fingers high, and a model was ordered to be kept in the court room as a standard of measurement. A special committee was appointed to keep track of the size of such bonnets in use.

The men of that period had fancies for silk scarfs and vests, wore lace on their cuffs, and sometimes came to church in things not considered proper for that service. Saddle decorations in silver or gold embroidery called for attention, but the wigs of men gave much concern to the court. This feature was sometimes too long, or stood too high above the forehead, and even the natural hair might be worn too long, as in the case of a preacher who was ·summoned in 1693. In this matter the long hand of the law was discovered by a man who was fined in December for a wig which he wore in April.

We learn from the records that women in 1693 wore long laces on their cuffs, had belts of brocard, feathers in their bonnets, and their hair dressed high. Along with these offenses the court was much engaged with cloaks which were too long. The casaque by law must not come below the knee, but maids and mistresses alike overlooked this measure, even in making a mourning veil. A baker's wife was brought to trial because her coat was so long that she could comfortably sit upon it (. . . *dass Sie völlig darauf sitzen könnte*). She was excused for this once.

In 1694 the Reformation-Chamber evidently sought the source of evil, by calling in various classes of tradesmen and making them take oath to obey the ordinances. Fifteen shoemakers swore they would make no shoes except of black calfskin, with heels not over two inches high and not pointed. Likewise, the tailors were bound to keep the law, the hoodmakers were forbidden to go to private houses to make hoods, and long injunctions were issued to wig-makers and the designers of the Bernese bonnets. All of these latter articles had been making trouble for the court for a long time. Away back in 1679 a ladies' hood was cut open and found stuffed with a basketful of shavings. (See Figure 16, page 59.)

During the ten years covered by this broken record from Bern more than 800 cases of dress were heard, a manifestation of the spirit as well as the diligence of a seventeenth-century tribunal. The ordinances continued to be renewed almost to the end of the eighteenth century, but unfortunately the record of prosecutions stops at 1696, and does not become available again until nearly a hundred years later. Only fragments from this interval have survived, and the investigator must wait till 1782 to find how the final fifteen years brought sumptuary regulations to a close.

XIII. ZURICH. REFORMATIONS-KAMMER, 1710

 THE proceedings of the Reformations-Kammer of Zurich for 1710 contain by far a greater number of cases heard in one year than are found in any of the three cities in the eighteenth century, and are here given to show the extreme to which prosecutions for sumptuary irregularities was carried. The minutes of that year must not be considered a common phenomenon nor as indicating a high average of court activity, for the statistics given on other pages show that while the laws continued in the statute books the execution sometimes fell to zero. Hence the year 1710 must be accepted as a period of high zeal for reform in these matters, induced by reasons which are not fully identified and not paralleled in the neighboring towns at the time.

Meeting forty-four times, once a week, on Tuesdays, with few exceptions, the chamber showed a diligence which must be commended. The court was composed of prominent citizens of whom those from the upper Small Council included the deputy burgomaster as president, four former gild masters, and two other members. Sitting with them from the Great Council were two former rural governors, a judge, and an ordinary member of this popular body. The following notes on their proceedings include both sumptuary cases and other matters which show the scope of their competence.

At the beginning of the year it was customary for the court to call the attention of its lower officials and the city police to their duties and to point out special delinquencies needing closer watch. So on January 7 they warned them that stricter observation should be given to Sunday occupations, and in particular to what people were doing during the evening services on Sunday, Wednesday, and Saturday, while taverns were warned to keep within the law. A company of young citizens who met at the Schwert inn would be cited for next Tuesday.

112

Cases began with a company of young men who met in a private house outside the city and danced with young women on a holiday (*Bechteli Tag*). Two students were referred to the school authorities for punishment. The wife of Jacob Rahn of the Red Eagle was cited for a new-fashioned evening dress and a bonnet with a large "bush." Frau Wagnerin, furrier, was held for a wide open dress collar. Two young ladies wore chains in church and were fined. Another young lady had cuffs with loosened seam (probably exposing her arm). Playing cards on Sunday and various misdemeanors cost Herr Lutziatorf and a party a substantial total in fines. Matthias Haffmeister, student, was held for wearing a neck-scarf, a large collar, a big fur muff, a long mantle, and colored breeches.

A member of the court was commissioned to look out for dancing and gambling in taverns and other places, and also to take note of women who wore bonnets (*Boden-Cappen*) at the evening services. It was further ordered that the coming together for talk by all sorts of persons, men, women, and young people at the door of the church after service must be stopped.

In February two young ladies named Engelfried were held for wearing silk jackets, bonnets with excessively large bush, white shoes, and also for disobedience to the ordinance against watching wedding processions and funerals. Herr Wüster's daughter wore unlawful cuffs, so did Sir Caspar Meissen's wife, Sir Heinrich Grebel's wife and the two daughters of ex-master of the mint, Herr Geiger. These two girls were also fined for costly muffs. Another lady appeared in church with an extra large *Tachli-Tüchli* and wore on the street a bonnet-hood with high-built ribbons thereon. Heinrich Meyer from Regensdorf had to pay two pounds for profanity and uttering a "flood of dissolute words against one of our citizens." Catherine Reynacher, a servant of Statthalter Dangler, was brought in for wearing in the street a forbidden headdress and cap. Esther Sprungli held a sort of housewarming for young women and butcher boys. A row ensued, and not only Esther but three girls, four butcher boys, and two men were put down for fines.

At this same session Frau Melchior Muralt, Heinrich Birchensperger's daughter, and trumpeter Steiner's daughter were all held for cuffs improperly open. The daughter of the sculptor Daniker wore white slippers, and Anna Barbara Liechtli, servant of Lieutenant Fäsi, had cords on her hood and large ribbons on her fur cap. Mrs. Conrad Kitter, wife of a sugar baker and daughter of sausage-maker Müller, wore fashionable clothing not suitable to her class, and was seen on the street in a low bonnet with a great "bush" of ribbons. Miller Klingler's maid was also seen in such a bonnet, Frau Bodmer's servant wore a costly hairpin and a knitted silk and wool coat, the Schonauer maid had a bonnet with ribbons and a silk scarf which reached to her knee, while the Werdmüller maid from upper Kirchgasse ventured out with lace and cords on her hood and dress collar. A waitress at the Schwert inn went to church in a forbidden headdress and a garnet ornament with a gold lock.

The twenty-fifth of February was a busy day, with nineteen cases requiring dress reform. Eight ladies had illegal cuffs, and the bonnets made nearly as much trouble. For wearing a camisole where it could be seen the daughters of schoolmaster Backofen, of a smith, of a miller, and of a cabinet-maker were among those brought to book. Catherine Riedhaar went to St. Jacob's church in a bonnet with great rosettes, an apron of silk-wool flor, and otherwise displayed her pride. Fräulein Werdmüller also went to this church not only with forbidden cuffs, but with large points on her church veil and a colored ribbon underneath the cap. Barbel Aster wore wide lace on white goods, two Orelli sisters appeared in cuffs, while their necks were displayed in a trifling way by wide dress collars, and Fräulein Ulrich of Niederdorf Gate had to account for a bushy bonnet and for curling and powdering her hair. Finally, Mrs. Müller, wife of accountant Müller, was admonished for her lack of regularity in going to church.

The month of March is not noted for agreeable weather in Zurich, yet the ladies were compelled to appear in court in large numbers, and some new fashions appear in the list of accusations. Lace cuffs attracted less attention, as only four or five cases were recorded, and only one man was cited for having a costly cloth coat with much fur on it. A maid from the Hirsch inn was out in an expensive camisole, a damask hat with ribbons, wide cords on her hood and dress

Fig. 41. Germany. Eighteenth Century.

collar, and was wearing a neck-ribbon. Another maid matched her by going to church in a marten-fur cap with ribbons on it, highly colored sleeves of silk, very modish, and a wide apron. Miss Hug wore edging on her church dress, with large and perforated cords about the collar. Sergeant Lindner's daughter had wide cords and a wrong camisole, while artist Schweizer's two daughters both wore broad cords, with their neck openings very scandalously wide. Three ladies had to appear, one for a silk flowered jacket, one for a silk jacket, and white shoes, and the other for a costly muff with very wide sable edging.

Certain maidservants would have made a picture together. Councilman Locher's maid wore in her costume a silver hairpin, had a wide open dress collar about which hung a highly colored scarf, her apron was red with large white fringes,

Fig. 42. France. Fontange Headdress, late 17th Century.
After Bonnard.

and she carried a book with silver mountings. Dr. Hottinger's maid was equipped with a sable cap with large ribbons, a damask bonnet also trimmed with wide ribbons, a peek-a-boo dress collar with wide open neck, a wide apron, a "flaming" scarf, wore corals with a gilt fastening, and carried a book trimmed with silver. Hirzel's maid was conspicuous in a very large felted scarf, a silver hair-needle with two rose ornaments, a cap with ribbons, and an East Indian apron (probably printed calico). Fräulein Ziegler wore a large *fontange*, the tall headdress from France. (Figure 42.) So did Frau Römer, but she also went out into the neighborhood in her camisole. Frau Elsinger was fined for wearing a dirty jacket, a most unusual case if it was dirt and not the jacket that was offensive. Another woman not only wore a camisole, but it had plush trimming an eighth of an ell wide. A cabinet-maker's wife and Council-clerk Meyer's daughter were seen outside wearing house-coats. Shearer Stadler's daughter had to pay for wearing cuffs on her sleeves. Two young women wore their jackets to St. Jacob's church. Fräulein Wolf and Frau Orelli wore chains about their necks in church, while Barbara Saltzmann had to appear for a beautiful jacket of blue burat, a gray silk dress with large white gauze scarf. Fräulein Hochzeiter was cited for a *fontange* headdress, with jacket and dress both of blue goods. Major Hirzel's wife was out of her house in the neighborhood in her *fontange* and jacket. A clerk from the Fraumünster church was called in for a powdered wig and otherwise ostentatious apparel. Two young ladies, as well as apothecary Lavater's wife, wore jackets unlawfully, and lockmaker Seyffer's daughter had cuffs which she ought not to have worn. Frau Werdmüller-an-der-Sill had a small gold neck-chain, but she wore it to church. Herr Pestalozzi's daughter wore both a neck-chain and cuffs in the house of worship. A house-coat on the street brought in Balber's daughter, while Fräulein Anna Magdelena Fries had to pay a large fine for a house-coat with a sash, costly rings, and a bonnet with a large "bush" of ribbons on it. Frau shoemaker Schauffelberger caused attention in a striped red house-jacket, as did Felix Grebel's daughter in a bonnet overdone with ribbons, and Captain Engelfried's maid with her collar scandalously wide open. The session of the eleventh of March closed by fining cabinet-maker Nozli's daughter for appearing in public in her jacket.

At the next meeting, Anna Schmidt of Setinmur, who was in service with Master Heinrich Locher, shopkeeper near the Katzenthor, was threatened with imprisonment for talking during the children's service in the Fraumünster church, and Diaconus Fries of St. Peter's was directed to examine the young woman and warn her that in future she must give proper attention. Catherine Werdmüller, in service with landvogt Hess was given a considerable fine for powdering her hair and wearing an unlawful house-jacket, with a bonnet ornamented with lace. Elizabeth Lähr, waitress with bailiff Esslinger of Otenbach, had large points on her sash, and appeared in a street-jacket, with wide cords on her hood and dress collar. Three other ladies had to pay for wearing house-jackets in public. Treasurer Bauer's wife went to the wedding of innkeeper Wirth with a gold neck-chain and a scarlet dress. Four other ladies wore bonnets with excess of ribbon clusters, while a house-coat and a street-jacket caught a fine, along with a neck-chain worn in church.

Not counting numerous police cases of Sunday and late-hour drinking, dancing, and going out of the city on the Sabbath, the month of April brought many dress offenders into court. Several house-jackets caused fines. Major Hirzel's daughter-in-law wore a very new-fashioned foreign silk cap, and on top of that a large *fontange* with rosettes. Five ladies apparently of good families had excessively large and provocative ribbon clusters on their bonnets. Mrs. candy-maker Kitter, who was a Miss Müller, attended the innkeeper wedding mentioned above and was too conspicuous in an expensive, fashionably embroidered neck-scarf. Herr Huber, student living in Rindermarkt Street, was held for his large collar, his open cassock, and for talking in church. When Herr Lavater held a bridal procession, the bride and all of the young ladies who rode in the line wore colored ribbons and had to appear in this court. Herr Kitt came out on Sunday in a bright scarlet mantle, and on the same day joined a drinking party whose names he refused to divulge. This cost him all together ten pounds.

The war upon periwigs was taken up in earnest on the tenth of April, when six men of high standing were brought before the court because of these costly white head-ornaments. The culprits included Pastor Seller's son, Gild-master Landolt, Captain Füssli, Secretary Bräm, Conrad Escher, and Johannes Landolt, who were assessed a small fine, and notice was given out that within a month citations would be issued against all wearers of this extravagance. This promise was actually fulfilled when nineteen men of the upper ranks were brought up on May 15 for wearing powdered wigs. In July, twenty-five more gentlemen were brought to court for the same offense, and, except for a

Fig. 43.   Basel.   Chevalier Schaub, by H. Rigaud.

couple of isolated cases, the matter rested till November, when Dr. Muralt, Dr. Hottinger, Dr. Ott, Major Wolf, District-Governor Hirzel, Herr Orell, and District-Governor Bram's son were all fined for powdered wigs. There this matter rested for the remainder of the year 1710. (Figure 43.)

The sessions of the Reformation-Chamber during the

summer of 1710 were occupied with many cases of scandal, street quarrels, drinking on Sunday and at late hours, dancing, going outside the city gates at forbidden hours on Sunday, driving to Baden on the Sabbath, card playing and card selling, and other matters in their minor police jurisdiction, but officials did not fail in their observation of the costume of their fellow citizens. The low bonnet with its high tower of ribbons, or the decorated hood felt the power of the law. The expensive street-coat, as well as the house-coat on the street were under observation, while powdered hair, neck-chains, and lace cuffs, sometimes singly and at others in a combination of all these evils, caused the wearers to appear in court. An over-embroidered scarf, white shoes at one time and red slippers at another with other improprieties were fined, and in some cases the court did not fail of words in describing offensive clothing, as when a young lady was held for powdering her hair, " wearing a pernicious large collar," and for " improper excessive ostentation." Major Meiss's two daughters appeared in " French hoods with black and yellow ribbon clusters thereon, breastpiece, French bodice with flaps hanging out over the apron, no dress collar, altogether French."

Social habits are perhaps visible in the case of a woman who threw dirty water out of her window and was let off with a severe reprimand, since no one was injured, but when a manservant living near the Kronen Thor did the same thing he doused Herr District-Secretary Heidegger, which was another matter. He answered that the accident was not intentional, but he was ordered to apologize on the spot and pay a fine of three pounds.

On Sunday, August 31, there was a meeting of the Triple Collegium, of which the minutes were recorded with those of the Reformation-Chamber. Those present included Antistes Klingler, superintending minister of the city, three other pastors, two archdeacons, two vice-governors of the town, two masters of gilds, rural governor Grebel, and Director Orelli. The subject for discussion was the moral condition of the community, and the outcome was a series of resolutions or complaints, " *Gravamina,*" on the existing situation, which give a little insight into the effect of the laws which we have been noting.

First, the Sabbath is profaned by drinking, and at hours forbidden by ordinance. There is neglect of the morning

Fig. 44.   Germany.   Eighteenth Century.

service for young people. In fact, children have been found playing dice at this hour in the fortification ditches of the city. Nursemaids and apprentices walk up and down the promenades and chatter when they should be in church. Meetings of workmen ought to be postponed till after evening service, to prevent interference with the hours of worship, and the church service held on Tuesdays is likewise badly attended.

Even on week-days taverns permit drinking beyond the lawful hours, and corner groggeries are matters of complaint. Mischief-makers at night are abroad, so that married ladies going with lanterns through the streets are hustled by bad boys. To stop this it is recommended that a watchman in plain clothes be appointed to attend to these miscreants so that women may go about the city without danger.

Ostentation in dress is increasing to excess. Fancy woolens, French bosoms, and the ribbon clusters on hoods and bonnets are getting deeply rooted. "Of other clothes there would be much to say but there was no improvement to be hoped for."

Card-playing is becoming very common among young and old, and especially in taverns people are playing without shame. Fifteen-year-old boys throw dice on the Lindenhof, and their cursing and swearing is disgusting. During market hours boys and girls are allowed to play in taverns, where market people have all sorts of games to get their money. This sort of thing should be stopped, and another bad practice is gaining rapidly where people play ninepins on the ramparts on Sunday.

The Collegium was also annoyed because too many young people follow funeral processions. They should be admonished from the pulpit to keep away from such occasions. Looking at other young men, complaint arises that candidates for the ministry and other students are wearing wigs and large collars; in fact, the greater part of them include false hair in their costume.

Finally, there are irregularities in the country parishes when these young people come to marry, for bridal parties are allowed to go from one parish to another for the ceremony, with only a note from the pastor instead of an official permission.

Whether this action of the Triple Collegium inspired greater diligence on the part of the Court of Reformation would be difficult to prove, but prosecutions went on with at least the accustomed vigor. The season for pleasant trips to Baden as a watering-place drew toward a close, but the watchful eye of the court found a whole group of ladies playing cards at that resort, and two or three men drove out

Fig. 45. Germany. Eighteenth Century.

there on Sunday. Cases of excess in costume rested somewhat for a month, although Herr Muralt had to pay the fines of three persons who attended his wedding, a young lady was held for her jacket, and Simler, Junior, student in theology, was too conspicuous in his shoulder mantel and taffeta garters.

A phase of welfare work also appears in a case which took

much space in the record, where a man complains that his wife is constantly under the influence of liquor (*überfüllt mit Wein*) and he appeals for help, requesting that the key of the cellar be taken away from her and given to him. The settlement of this housewifely prerogative and its unfortunate consequences was placed in the hands of a committee of pastors and others, who were directed to demand the key and give it to the husband. Over him was hung a penalty of fifty pounds if he let her have it, but he must arrange for the opening of the food cellar for midday and evening meals. By this plan it was hoped to keep her within the bounds of moderation, and the scheme was to be re-enforced by an official appeal to lead a better life. The result is not on record.

The autumn season brought out costumes and garments which gave the court fresh activity. Conspicuous among the offenders were the wearers of lace cuffs, characterized at one point as "innovations" and persistently fined. Inside of a period of four weeks in October and November twenty-nine women, twelve of them at one session, were called in for this over-decoration of their sleeves. Still worse was the trouble with the jacket, for which thirty-seven women, seventeen at one session and thirteen at once at another, were called to account during the same months. Sometimes this offense was combined with bonnet troubles or white shoes, but there seemed to be a determined warfare on cuffs and jackets, followed closely by the persecution of the bushes of ribbon which adorned the fashionable flat hats.

A few other kinds of unlawful dress appeared during these last months. One lady wore a red breastpiece decorated with gilt passementerie, as well as lace cuffs and an "annoying bush" on her head. Two young sisters were brought in because one wore a jacket just like her dress and the other a garment of damask. Colored ribbons at a wedding, along with a silk coat, were fined again, as well as gold ornaments on a camisole. Carrying a book bound in tortoise-shell to church drew a round penalty, however serious may have been the piety of the owner, but the Christmas month meetings were devoted mostly to the punishment of street fights and quarrels more or less serious.

This busy year 1710 saw at least 523 cases pass before the Reformation-Court, of which 317 were for wrong garments or personal ornaments. Two hundred and forty-seven women and seventy men appeared in this grave tribunal during the forty-four sessions, a record which was never reached again during the century. The promulgation of sumptuary laws, as well as prosecutions for disobedience, continued, but with irregular displays of energy. The objects of attack among articles of dress changed as time went on, and some of these deserve a little more attention.

XIV. END OF THE EIGHTEENTH CENTURY

THE Reformation-Chamber of Basel was busy in 1727, as the record of forty-one meetings shows that 210 women were presented for unlawful costume in some form. The efforts of the court were nearly all spent on correcting servants who aspired to appear in fashionable forms, or in garments above their class. French styles were invading Switzerland, and the authorities insisted that Basel dress, not foreign fashions, should be followed. Only nine men had to appear, and these were seen with fringes or cords on their hats. The balance of the 283 cases was nearly taken up with the forty-six charges against people who went outside the gates on Sunday. Silks, laces, silver fringes, hoop-skirts, and powdered hair figured as formerly, but ninety-three of the accused were dismissed.

Six years later, in 1733, this leniency was even greater, for out of a total of 209 delinquents 106 were excused on various grounds. Yet ninety-eight women and five men appeared to have had something wrong with their clothing, while spending Sunday outside the gates in walking, or in boating on the Rhine, or in dancing at some country resort brought a summons to ninety-one more. Again the servants, cited for lace and hoods, were the chief sufferers. The hoop-skirt was frequently prosecuted, but this article was affected only by the upper classes, and the cases were fewer. The next year, however, the court met once a month, and every citation for women's dress was against the forbidden crinoline. By 1737 the fashion had gone so far that the court could only decree that women be warned against the growing custom of making the hoop-skirt *too large and wide.* Later the chamber noted that short mantles were making great headway and ordered the constables to report the wearers. Referring the matter of footwear to the city council as the highest authority, both courts gravely agreed that gold and silver ornaments on slippers were forbidden by the ordinance.

For various transgressions in dress in 1737, fifty-one women and only eight men were summoned to court. Sunday dancing and unlawful passing out of the gates on the Sabbath accounted for eighty-six more cases, so that one can observe the direction of the energy of the constables, but when it is noted that one hundred and twenty-two persons out of the one hundred and fifty-two summoned are dismissed with or without censure, the remaining thirty cases do not leave an impression of severity. In fact, from this point on the activity of the Reformation-Chamber except for momentary revivals was gradually withdrawn from the censorship of dress into the other forms of social supervision.

In Zurich in 1728 the attack on clothing began in earnest in June, and the offenses were all committed by women. During previous years a few cases of exposed neck had appeared in the court docket, but now a fresh severity toward that fashion became evident. Action in that direction was accentuated by the report of the Triple Collegium of June 6 made to the mayor and city council, to the effect that it was highly necessary to proceed against "clothing and pride ruinous to the country," and in particular against the fashionable "highly offensive uncovering of the neck, very displeasing to God and the respectable world" (*Höchst ägerliche, Gott und der ehrbaren Welt sehr misfällige Entblössung um den Hals*). Women not only appear in the house of the Lord in this alluring exhibition but they also let themselves be seen about the city, and the consequences are to be feared if this offense is not pursued vigorously by ordinance and punishment.

Whatever may have been the incitement to action, some fifty-eight ladies were brought into court that year for illegal articles of clothing. On one day in November, nineteen, and on another, twelve women at a time had to answer for costume, a large number because of a lack of covering for their necks. Yet it is evident that sumptuary prosecutions, although large, formed only a diminishing part of the business of the

court, for in that same year an even hundred were held for
disorderly conduct or slander, and nineteen for other offenses.

The records of the Reformation-Chamber of Bern for the
eighteenth century have been preserved only in fragments,
except for the years 1782 to 1797. During those fifteen years

Fig. 46.   Germany.   Eighteenth Century.

severe restrictions were repeatedly issued, but prosecutions
under them were rare. Four women were cited for dress in
1783, and one man had to appear in 1785, otherwise the
sessions were chiefly occupied with dancing, gambling, and
servants for leaving service. Warnings about articles of costume were sometimes printed in the *Wochenblatt*, the weekly
publication used for official decrees, but no court actions
were taken.

In 1784, a dozen years before the close of its functions, the Chamber on the sixteenth of June sent a long communication to the city council stating that the court had done its best to enforce the sumptuary ordinances. It had maintained

Fig. 47. Germany. Eighteenth Century.

secret observers, had held officials strictly to their duties, and often warned the public regarding the law. "But all in vain" (*Aber alles vergebens*). "The very rare informations touched for the most part the person of no means of the working class, and were not always right." Prominent people had not been reported in a long time, for no one appeared to see anything wrong with them, yet it was evident that all over the city the Reformation ordinance was daily and in nearly every provision openly and boldly disregarded. As to how long the situation should thus continue to exist was left to the action of the city council. Fifteen months later one man, a postillion, was tried and fined for wearing gold epaulettes and braid on his waistcoat, and the war in Bern was over.

XV. CONCLUSIONS

THE results of this warfare of centuries against fashion in dress have already been indicated and will be further summarized in the tables of statistics which follow in the appendix. The end can be clearly seen in the arrival of the French Revolution, which not only caused great political disturbances, but liberalized the laws in favor of individual freedom. Switzerland was affected like the rest by these movements. Torn by the invasion of French armies, reconstructed temporarily as an Helvetic Republic, then returned to its place as a confederation with old outlines but new liberties, its statesmen were busy with wars and external relations more than with personal regulations. The preservation of their political existence was more important than rules for the dress which the people might choose to wear. Costume did not violently change at once, but laws about it, already disregarded and unenforced, ceased to encumber the statutes.

Reasons for the marked variation of enforcement observed in the earlier centuries are more difficult to ascertain. Occasionally internal disturbances explain the lack of attention, but the spurts of vigor which carry prosecutions into fifties and hundreds of cases are not so easily accounted for. Such energy rarely occurs at the same time in any two cities, and cannot well be ascribed to general revivals of virtue. The governments being aristocratic in form, the changes in officials occurred only at long intervals, and the rise of new political parties bent on the preservation of Swiss habits and costume is out of the question.

That city councils occasionally woke up suddenly to strike at the invasion of new fashions and pursued the innovators with heavy fines is perfectly evident, but one would hesitate to enumerate the local causes of such energetic action. That Swiss citizens should maintain their own costume as a patriotic duty, that ranks and classes should be distinguished

131

by their dress, were rock-bound principles throughout, so far as laws were concerned. Economic reasons were reiterated without end, for the prevention of extravagance in display was deemed a governmental duty, both in times of general distress and in periods of prosperity. Protection of home industry occasionally appeared in so many words, when articles of Swiss handiwork were definitely prescribed, but the motives are so deeply interwoven that cost and social welfare must also be taken into consideration.

Life in the narrow streets of an old town of ten thousand people was far different from that of today. Foreign commerce existed but was fed by the products of hand-looms and hammers instead of factories and forges. Moderate wealth, as we should regard it today, was accumulated by a few merchants and landowners, while the common people worked out their livelihood in their small stores and work-shops. Yet, in spite of the diminutive size of these occupations, they were dutifully and minutely regulated by the local government. In the seventeenth century every trade in Basel lived under a code of prices so complete and comprehensive that it puts to shame the modern American experiment.

All this emphasizes once more the fact that laws governing personal expenditure and the form of dress were not extraordinary, tentative measures, but regulations which have their rightful place in the conceptions of that day. The same methods were followed in other independent cities of Europe, and the Swiss towns were therefore not alone in careful prescriptions for the conduct and costume of their inhabitants.

That the ordinances constantly failed to get complete obedience is revealed in the preambles of these laws as they were renewed at intervals a few years apart. The sad tones of the lawmakers may have been due in part to official pessimism meant to scare their constituents into good behavior, but it is clear from the records of the courts that the dictates of fashion were more powerful than the orders of councils. This condition is confirmed by the changes made from time to time in the provisions of the ordinances. Absolute prohibition of a garment or form declared in one law is later modified by an amendment which permits the use of it provided the shape or material is made to follow the directions then and there provided. Later still, even these restrictions may disappear, either because fashion has prevailed, or the object went out of style.

To the end of our period the ordinances were frequently revised and renewed, although the last half-century showed far less a desire to prescribe minutely the articles of costume. This persistence, whatever other motives they may have had, saved the face of the lawmakers, who felt obliged to make some public declaration on the subject, but the same people when sitting in a court of justice practically admitted the victory of fashion. Prosecutions faded and ceased with the law still shouting from the books.

Centuries of experience seemed to teach these city councils little or nothing as to the actual nature of sumptuary law. They persisted in the attempt to make people follow their rules long after England had ceased to regulate dress, yet Basel, Bern, and Zurich were in respectable contemporary company, and should not be singled out for reproval. From their experiences a long essay on the value of governmental regulation of dress, or food, or funerals might follow here, but the reader is left to his own conclusions.

APPENDIX

CONTENTS OF APPENDIX

STATISTICAL CHARTS

Title Page, Bern Ordinance 1708.

Original 6½ x 4¼.

I. ZURICH. EXTRACT FROM THE ORDINANCE OF 1628

Ostentation

And since ostentation in clothing on all sides is taking more and more the upper hand and is becoming so much in vogue both among high and low classes of men and women that no one is dressed according to his rank, and many are suffering in household and business while wife and child are spending so much on superfluity and costliness in clothing and often in furniture, trumpery and bed-clothing, therefore we warn everybody, man or woman, most earnestly and publicly, that they avoid all costliness and superfluity especially in ostentatious clothing, and in particular that they abstain from all foreign fashions, and in future set no more gold or silver cords on their clothing, but let everyone apply and use the common, honorable clothing customary in our country, suitable to every class and more becoming to us, since through such frivolous and foreign dress the frivolous heart and mind will be perceived.

Therefore we warn and command most earnestly all parents, women or men, not to permit their children or servants to show such ostentation, costliness and new fashions, otherwise where it occurs, we shall hold the parents or fathers of family responsible who allow such conduct by their children or servants.

Inasmuch as we have ordered that everyone in city and country hold to honorable dress suitable to his rank we shall maintain anew a diligent oversight of these things, and especially shall at once give warning not only to persons who are clothed contrary to their class and to the previous ordinances, but also to the workers who make these things and to the merchants who bring new forms into the country, or demand from those who do not take advice the established fines and thus prevent the beginnings in time.

REFORMATIONS

Ordnung

Welche in
Lobl. Stadt Basel/
Von
Einem Ehrs. Grossen Rath
Zu
Pflantzung der Ehrbarkeit/ und Ausreutung aller-
hand eingeschlichener Mißbräuchen/
Dero
Burgern/ Angehörigen und unter dero Schutz stehenden
vorgeschrieben worden/
ANNO M DCC XXVII.

V. Buch Mosis XXIII, 14.
Dein Lager soll heilig seyn/ daß kein Schand unter dir gesehen werde/und
der HERR dein GOtt sich von dir wende.

Gedruckt bey Johann Heinrich Decker.

Title Page, Basel Ordinance 1727.
Original 9¼ x 5¾.

II. BASEL. ORDINANCE 1637

INTRODUCTION TO SECTION ON CLOTHING

Therefore, (alas) it is sufficiently well known how in many men and women, young and old, high rank and low and their children, both luxuriousness and ostentation in clothing have so taken root and increased that not only is honor repressed and no condition or rank can be recognized, but experience shows that when such useless, excessive ostentation and cost is not remedied and suppressed in good time, the Almighty God (to whom such a thing is most highly offensive and who punishes it every time, as we have examples enough in the holy scripture) will be still more violently angered and may bring upon us all heavier and harder punishments and distress. To this daily experience up to now has shown that through seductive, pernicious and excessive ostentation and pride many persons have suffered decrease and loss of food, yea, at last fallen into extreme poverty and want, therefore, we, as a Christian Government, holding office in the sight of Almighty God, not only recognize our duty to abolish the said excessive magnificence, but also in praise and honor of the faithful and merciful God, we have firmly and steadfastly undertaken to plant and propagate all modesty as far as possible, and to so direct things that all destructive superfluity may be checked.

Therefore let our beloved citizens hereby take warning so that everyone in his own household for himself, his wife, children and the servants entrusted to his care, put aside and refrain from great extravagant pride and conspicuous unnecessary cost, but rather use modesty and the honesty well-pleasing to God the Lord. Therefore in this follow God's gracious will rather than evil desires, but especially let all men and each one in particular submit to the ordinance which follows in dutiful obedience and subjection.

[Here follow specific orders respecting dress and expense.]

Mandat vnd Ordnungen
Vnserer gnedigen Herren,

Burgermeister / klein vnd grosser Rähten
der Statt Zürich :

Vß ihren fürnemsten alten Mandaten / zu mehrer befür-
derung / eines insonderheit zu disen letsten vnd schweren zyten / hoch erfor-
derten büßfertigen Läbens vnd ehrbaren wandels / zusamen gezogen / vnd vff die erst-
nüwlich sich erzeigten vngewohnten vil Erdbidem / widerumb erneüweret / noht-
wendigklich verbesseret / auch in der Statt vnd Landschafft offentlich ver-
kündt / vnd zu männigklichesse mehrer nachricht in
Truck verfertiget.

Im M DC L. Jahre.

Title Page, Zurich Ordinance 1650.
Original 6½ x 4¾.

III. ZURICH. ORDINANCE 1650

EXTRACT ON OSTENTATION

Then we observe and experience with special sorrow, sad to say, that in spite of these more and more grievous times ostentation in dress and all kinds of fashionable novelties and superfluities, against which for the good of the citizens at large and the whole country we in time past have enacted earnest prohibitions and well-meant ordinances, have so taken the upper hand in all ranks in city and country that no one appears clothed according to his class, yea, even minor children are thrust into the greatest display from the cradle up, all of which things in the pure and holy eyes of God are a horrible abomination and therefore it is badly to be feared that unless people desist therefrom and openly and without hypocrisy reform, the wrath of God will break over us heavily. Besides this many a man in his household and activities will badly suffer when he and his wife and child carry on such pride, superfluity and costliness in clothing and often in furniture, frippery and bed-drapery, and even among maid-servants themselves so great a display has existed that one can hardly recognize their class any more.

Consequently we have looked upon it as a specially great necessity to revive and sharpen the ordinances formerly made against pride, display and expense. On this account we command with great earnestness and under heavy penalty that every person in city or country, whether cleric or layman, high class or low, woman or man, young or old, burger or peasant, attend to and use the clothing befitting his class both at home and abroad, especially at Baden, and on the other hand entirely put aside and avoid all sumptuousness of foreign form, innovations, superfluities and splendour (since in these things only the trifling heart and spirit of a man will be perceived).

[Continued by elaborate directions for avoidance or use of materials.]

IV. NUREMBERG. CLOTHING ORDINANCE, 1693

INTRODUCTION

Since the Most Noble, Foresighted and Mostwise Council of the City of Nuremberg of the Holy Roman Empire with displeasure is obliged to observe and learn by experience to what extent the salutary clothing ordinance renewed in the year 1657 is almost frivolously and contemptuously forgotten by the majority of citizens, and in these troublesome times with the lack of food are addicted to excessive costly display, to the no small vexation of virtue loving persons, so that one can hardly distinguish one class from another, whereby observing foreigners of high or low degree in travelling through are often annoyed, not to mention that GOD the Almighty Creator and Preserver of mankind for these and their other sins often threatens to plunge whole cities and lands into ruin, wherefore they have made a better clothing ordinance which shall go into effect at the coming Easter.

THE FIRST RANK

First for all men belonging to the first rank it is allowed to wear hat cords of solid and spun gold, but these must not exceed 20 to 25 *gulden* in value. On the other hand for them to wear hat-cords set with costly precious stones is of course forbidden. Further they may wear caps of velvet with tirmmings of marten fur. Wigs shall not exceed 8 to 10 *thaler* in value. Their collars and facings, or in their place scarfs together with the Handtätzlein, with or without lace, sewed or worked shall not exceed 12 to 15 *thaler* in worth. Also they are allowed to wear jackets as well as mantles made of any kind of silk goods, as brocade, flowered satin, except smooth velvet, and the lined jackets and mantles at the most shall be lined with back-fur of marten or velvet.

Persons of the first rank may wear breeches, waistcoats and coats of velvet, satin and other garments made of silk, such as taffeta, or brocade, and also may use stockings wholly of silk. But they must avoid all other costly raiment, especially camisoles of gold and silver material, or made of gold and silver pieces (the value of which may run to 20 *thaler*) embroidered borders, long costly silk laces and excessive borders on clothing. They may wear on their waistcoats and coats silver and gilded buttons, likewise on a leather or woolen suit two silver or gold galoons, the lace and borders of which weigh one *loth*. [two ounces.] per ell. Seven ells for the border of a mantle is allowed. On the other hand they are earnestly forbidden to wear any excess of gold and silver, especially gold and silver embroidered sword-hangings worth more than 12 to 15 *thaler*, as well as too large gold and silver fringes on the gloves. Furthermore they are allowed to have gilded, silvered or damascened arms, such as pommel, cross and sheath point, but no excess of this kind may be carried.

Doctors, advocates and others will so regulate their dress according to their class that they do not conflict with the city laws and ordinances. And even though the old noble families eligible to the Council have had the privilege from old times down, yet no one else is allowed to have gold chains, gold hat-bands, nor silver-gilt buttons on their waistcoats, jackets and coats. On the other hand none of these (except members of the Council) shall have the right to wear any gold chains which exceed 120 *Rheingulden* in weight or value.

Further it is allowed and permitted for them to have horse outfits of leather with only gilded and silvered rings and buckles, saddles of leather with woolen or velvet seats, a woolen blanket not excessive in length, ornamented somewhat with fringes, gold lace, or cords, pistol holsters with velvet covers. Long embroidered saddle covers and similar pistol holsters as well as solid silver horse outfits are entirely forbidden. They may also have one or more colored brushes or pompons on the head-gear of their coach horses but in hanging on *dollen* [cloth flaps] or similar ornaments they must go to no excess. *Dollen* of whole or half silk are forbidden.

As to the horse ridden by a bride ribbons are allowed to the First Class to be used in the foretop, mane and tail; to the Second Class in the foretop and tail without the mane; and to the Third Class only the foretop, and to these last only a single color or ribbon.

It is forbidden to line the interior of coaches, chaises or caleches with silk or brocade, or to decorate them with costly fringes or *dollen*. They must not have superfluous gold ornaments on their sleighs. Outside of the First Class which from old times has had the right to use sleighs, whoever wishes to use this vehicle may not decorate the sleigh at all with gold, but may have some small amount of silver, but costly bells, feathers, silk *dollen* and other ornaments together with the sleigh valued at more than 100 or 120 *gulden* are entirely forbidden. At the same time these latter persons are reminded that in accordance with ancient custom when they purpose to go sleigh-riding they must give notice in advance to the ruling Burgermaster and request permission.

11

Whoever acts contrary to the points included above shall be liable to ten *gulden* penalty for each offense.

WOMEN AND YOUNG WOMEN OF THE OLD NOBLE FAMILIES

The women and young women of the First Rank may wear velvet hoods, but not too large, trimmed with sable or marten fur, which they may ornament only for honor occasions [weddings] or feast-days with gold roses or buckles and somewhat with pearls, but no diamonds. Such ornamentation must not exceed 70 to 75 crowns in gold. Likewise they are allowed to wear all gold hair-caps but without pearls, worth not over 30 to 40 *gulden* in coin. On the other hand it is forbidden to them to set diamonds in their hat-cords (if these come into use again) or in their hair-caps, but gold and other precious stones are allowed. Young women will be permitted to wear pearl hair-ribbons, or in place of them a head dress with gold ribbons as a coife.

And since great display and excess has hitherto been displayed in over long collars the women of this class are reminded that in future they must refrain from wearing such superfluously long and thick collars, and likewise the facings and specially the costly laces on them.

For bosom pieces they may use good velvet, satin, damask, as well as silk goods worked in with silver and gold, and even may trim these articles with all-gold laces or galoons. On the other hand they must totally abstain from goods worked only with gold and gold flowers. Further they are permitted to use figured or unfigured velvet, satin, damask or other silk goods for their coats and apron trimmings, but they are not entitled to have the coats bordered with excessive gold.

They may make their small mantles of satin, rosat, damask, budesoy, tabby, and place on them marten or other equally costly velvet trimmings. Also line them with marten fur, either one-sixth of an ell wide with the same goods turned over, or when one-fourth of an ell wide trim them with silk borders or laces. On the other hand it is entirely forbidden to wear mantellets of velvet, or any with sable, velvet, satin, or other costly linings, or with embroidered borders.

Women and young women of the highest rank may wear dresses of satin, damask, double taffeta and other silk goods, whether flowered or not flowered and it is permitted them to border or fasten on the dress or apron gold or silver galoons or similar laces of which the ell is not over two ounces in weight. On the other hand dress or aprons of gold or silver goods, or made of velvet trimmed with embroidered edges are strictly forbidden.

It is further permitted to this class to have a long gold chain worn not more than double with a seemly jewel or net-work, likewise, as has been their custom from old times, a gold neck-band and fastening, also gold neck-chains, although except for a jewel or pendant thereon no precious stones may be attached. They may also have neck ornaments of so-called " health-stones," also gold bracelets, although not more than one pair may be worn at a time, or in place of these small gold chains. Likewise they must avoid shoes and slippers bordered or embroidered with gold and silver under the penalty established below.

The wives of doctors and advocates may also wear clothing, ornaments, chains, gold rings and other things appropriate to their rank, provided that therewith they do not overstep the clothing ordinance and thereby exhibit their honor and birth with more than excessive display.

As often as anyone in the first rank offends against one or more of the points included above that person shall be obliged to pay ten *gulden* penalty for every offense, and more according to circumstances.

THE SECOND RANK

Clothing and costume of people in honorable trade and commerce, who have no open business, but for themselves with their own substance carry on conspicuous, courageous transactions and crafts at their own risk and hazard, and also those who have inherited from their ancestors the right to be in the aforesaid rank of the Grand Council.

Whatever is prohibited for wearing by persons of the uppermost rank is still more forbidden for this class. They may, however, wear hat-cords of silver only, or mixed with some gold, the value of which is not over six *gulden*, likewise galoons or laces of silver mixed one-half with gold on cloth or leather garments. Otherwise they shall entirely avoid wearing all other gold whether good or Leonisch.

Their hoods shall be of good smooth or ornamented velvet and the trimming of marten fur, but with no costly lining or trimming. Their facings with the so-called " acorns," or, in their place the neck-bands, together with the *Handtätzlein* with or without lace, must not exceed 12 or 15 *gulden* in value. Further they are permitted to wear a coat or mantle of woolen cloth lined with marten back fur, or without lining a simple mantle of taffeta, rosat, or wholly of silk, but this unwatered; for collars and trimmings three ells of velvet and no more. On the other hand they must avoid smooth velvet and other flowered silk goods.

They are permitted to have breeches, camisoles, and coats of satin, damask, taffeta and other silk goods, but to clothe themselves in good smooth velvet is forbidden. On their weapons they may have a silver or silver-plated cross, pommel and sheath point, but must avoid shoe-strings set with precious stones. They may have made horse outfits, saddles, pistol holsters of leather or woolen cloth, but not made of either good or bad velvet, nor may they carry any ribbons or superfluous buckle work, nor any reins made of gold or silver cords. Likewise it is entirely forbidden for the Second Rank to clothe their servants in livery and to trim their coats with borders for this purpose, or to use these when coach riding, though they may have coats for their servants made with one border and a cord of one color on them. Pompons on carriages and horses, also all gold and silver fringes on the horse outfit are forbidden. Coaches shall be lined with common cloth but not red or blue nor decorated with silk fringes.

DRESS OF WIVES AND DAUGHTERS OF MERCHANTS OF SECOND RANK

[Freely translated and condensed.]

Garments are the same as those of the women of the first rank, except that velvet hoods must not cost more than 24 *gulden*. They may have no gold buckles or gold lace but may wear articles made of gold and silver mixed. Caps with gold embroidery and so-called feather caps are forbidden, but they may wear silk caps with a narrow gold border, yet hats with gold or silver buckles as well as gold and silver chains and gold caps for the hair are forbidden. Collars with or without lace are limited to 12 to 16 *gulden*, otherwise they may be the same as for the first rank.

Doublets may be the same as for the first rank but not of velvet and may have ornaments of silver or silver worked with gold in lace or borders, but not all gold. Gold cords and chains are forbidden. Mantles may be made of taffeta, terzenell, camelshair or silk, but not flowered, watered or smooth silk. They may have facings or reveres of velvet skin and velvet, silk or lace borders one-sixth of an ell wide. No costly flowered material may be used. Gowns permitted are the same as for the first class except that they must not be made of plain silk velvet, cut or uncut, but flowered velvet may be used for this garment.

The wives and young women whose husbands and fathers belong to this class are allowed to wear cloaks lined with marten fur, and the cloaks may be made of watered camelshair cloth with a border of red or other colored velvet five-fourths of an ell wide but without lace or edging. They may wear aprons of taffeta, but only the unwatered, or camlet and other smooth silks when not flowered material with one border of silver mixed with a little gold, but more costly goods such as brocade, satin, etc., as well as Venetian and English scarlet and the French mode of wearing a train (whatever name they may call it) all are strictly forbidden.

At weddings women of this class may wear a simple long gold chain worth 75 to 80 gold crowns, a neck chain costing 25 to 30 crowns, with one stone set in gold (except diamonds, rubies and sapphires because it is difficult to tell real stones from false). A pearl pendant worth 25 to 30 *gulden* may be worn if not set with more than four pearls, otherwise all pearl chains and necklaces, all gold bracelets with or without stones, all pendants set with costly or imitation jewels worn upon the bare throat or otherwise, and particularly the so-called side chainlets are entirely forbidden.

The wives of doctors, advocates and doctors of medicine will follow the rules for the first rank and the fines are the same.

THIRD RANK

Costume of tradesmen and merchant people considered qualified for the Grand Council, having their own business but not so prominent and important, with or without agents, including also artisans eligible to the Small Council.

They are forbidden to wear gold, good or bad, or anything that looks like it. They may wear hat cords of silver costing not more than three or four *gulden*. Their hats may be of fur or figured velvet; their collars, with or without lace must not exceed ten *gulden* in value. Coats and mantles must be of woolen cloth, or of " ferrentum " or other half-silk material and lined with inferior fur. Facings, collars and cuffs can be of figured velvet, damask or taffeta, but linings of marten fur or smooth velvet plush are forbidden. Breeches and jackets may be of damask and inferior silk material, but satin, good figured velvet, cut or uncut, are totally forbidden under penalty of ten *gulden*.

To keep coaches, horses, chaises and caleches is strictly prohibited. If anyone needs to drive he may keep a coach by paying fifty *thaler* a year, but the vehicle must have no painting or carving on it and be lined with gray cloth. The horses are not to wear harnesses with silver or bright metal fixtures, while coachmen and servants cannot wear livery but be dressed in dark coats of plain gray without cords or borders.

WIVES AND DAUGHTERS OF THE THIRD RANK

These, including the wives of foreign clergy and school-masters, and daughters who live with their parents, may wear hoods of cut or uncut velvet with borders of dyed fur of marten, otter or jennet, and headdresses set with silver not exceeding ten *gulden* in price. Summer hats with silver hat-cords costing three to four *gulden* and silk headdresses with silver or mother of pearl bangles may be worn. Gloves may have silver lace on them but there must be no gold or anything that looks like it in hat-bands or headdresses. The latter are to be fastened with a silver galoon not too wide. Collars with or without lace and reveres up to six or eight *gulden*, or heavy collars worth ten or twelve *gulden* may be worn but must not be too high or too wide.

Brides of this class may wear black, green or nail-colored cloaks of camelot with velvet borders one ell wide. Gowns may be made of damask or other silk material but not satin or velvet, nor must they be adorned with "unnecessary frizzled lace."

Skirts and aprons of Turkish scarlet or half-silk material, smooth without flowers, with silk lace three fingers wide may be worn, but Venetian and English scarlet are forbidden. Mantles of unwatered camelot, or smooth camelshair may have facings of damask or other inferior goods, with lace not too wide, or a border of velvet or silk one-sixth of an ell wide.

Chains over the dress and pendants of real stones are forbidden but

a small chain about the neck of this width

weighing twelve to fourteen crowns and worth thirty to thirty-six *gulden* may be worn without a pendant. Permitted also is a necklace of *Elendsklauen* [poverty claws] or other single colored but not costly stones, as jasper, cornelian, etc., worth twenty-eight to thirty *gulden.* A silver belt (Leib-oder Tanzgürtel) costing eleven or twelve *gulden* is allowed, but unnecessary costly rings are forbidden and a fine of ten *gulden* is the penalty for breaking any of these rules.

FOURTH RANK

Clothing and fashions of mercantile people who began business within a few years, and those having few overseers and not yet included in the foregoing ranks, as also the shopkeepers and craftsmen who are in the aforesaid class, and all merchant clerks.

These persons are forbidden to have all the things denied to members of the first three classes. They may wear caps of figured mock-velvet with rims and linings of fur but not of marten. In case of mourning they may not wear crepe veils which are too long on their hats. These must not be more than four ells in length. They may wear collars and reveres of lace not exceeding three or four *gulden* in value. They may have woolen mantles with velvet collars, while breeches, coat, waistcoat and jacket may be of light silk.

The fine for wearing velvet, satin, etc. unlawfully is six *gulden* for each piece each time worn.

Included in this class also are imperial notaries, procurators and other secretaries of this kind.

V. BASEL. TAX ORDNUNG 1646

SPECIMEN CODES FOR SOME OF THE SEVENTY-EIGHT TRADES

HAT MAKER'S TAX.

HIGH HATS OF THE BEST PURE WOOL.			MEDIUM WOOL.		
A large man's hat	2 lb.	5 sh.	A large man's hat	1 lb. 1 sh. 8 d.	
One somewhat smaller	1 lb.	15 sh.	One somewhat smaller	16 sh. 8 d.	
One of medium size	1 lb.	5 sh.	One of medium size	13 sh. 4 d.	
One of small size		16 sh.	A boy's hat	7 sh. 6 d.	
A boy's hat		12 sh. 6 d.			
One still smaller		8 sh.			

PURE WOOL STRASSBURG HATS.			MEDIUM QUALITY WOOL.	
A large Strassburger hat	1 lb.	10 sh.	A large Strassburg hat	1 lb.
One somewhat smaller	1 lb.	5 sh.	One somewhat smaller	15 sh.
One of medium size	1 lb.		One of medium size	12 sh.
A child's hat		12 sh.	A child's hat	9 sh.

COARSE WOOL.

A large Strassburg hat	16 sh.	One of medium size	10 sh.
One somewhat smaller	13 sh. 4 d.	A child's hat	6 sh. 8 d.

SUNDGAUER HATS OF PURE WOOL.		MEDIUM QUALITY WOOL.	
One large	1 lb.	One large hat	12 sh. 6 d.
A smaller one	15 sh.	One smaller	10 sh.
Medium size	12 sh. 6 d.	One medium size	8 sh.

COARSE WOOL.

One large hat	8 sh.
One smaller	6 sh.
One medium size	5 sh.

BASEL HATS.

A klopfte hat of good pure wool	1 lb. 15 sh.

SEWED BASEL HATS.

A sewed Basel hat of finest and purest English stockings	4 lb.
Same made of Leyden stockings	3 lb. 10 sh.
Same made of Parisian stockings	2 lb.
When stockings are furnished the best English will sell at	1 lb. 10 sh.
Same with Leyden stockings and for lower quality	15 sh.

BASEL TAILOR TAX.

For a civilian suit of any material twice stitched or made with a cord. 2 lb. 10 sh.

For a suit made entirely smooth. 2 lbs.

For a cloth mantle with velvet collar lined above and in front. 1 lb. 15 sh.

For a summer cloak of buffi or other material twice stitched and lined above and front. 1 lb. 15 sh.

For a Council Member coat thrice stitched and bordered with satin 4 lb. and more according as the coat is made.

For a Judge's coat twice stitched. 3 lb. 10 sh.

For a mourning coat twice stitched. 3 lb. 5 sh.

For a civilian casaque of cloth made smooth for the furrier. 1 lb.

For a cloak for a bride with velvet on the figure and sleeves. 5 lb.

For a woman's cloak of the best make. 4 lb. 10 sh.

For a pair of sleeves of herrensagen or other material trimmed with double gold lace. 15 sh.

For a triple cloth apron edged all around. 6 sh.

For a woman's jacket of any material edged all around. 16 sh. 8 d.

For a cloth or skin jacket bordered with corduroy. 12 sh. 6 d.

An unmarried tailor when he works in the house of a customer gets for the day 2 sh. 6 d.

[After eighteen items of children's clothing there follow]

A woolen shirt for a man fitted in front and on the sleeves with buttons and lace. 1 lb.

A plain woolen shirt. 10 sh.

A pair of cloth stockings with cross stitch or double quilted for a man. 5 sh.

A night dress of burat, buffi, or other material made smooth. 1 lb.

As to the bosom pieces the labor cannot well be fixed because they are not alike and made in many different ways, the government makes certain against the master tailors that they shall not take from any one an excessive wage or they may expect punishment.

Especially for a woman's bosom made cheaply without flaps, having lace fastened with whalebone and attached to a undercoat not more shall be demanded than 8 sh. 4 d.

For a young woman the same trimmed with flaps or cords around the bosom and waist. 12 sh. 6 d.

VI. BASEL. SESSIONS OF THE REFORMATION CHAMBER

Year	Sessions	Year	Sessions	Year	Sessions	Year	Sessions
1674	4	1705	18	1736	12	1767	10
1675	18	1706	5	1737	31	1768	6
1676	13	1707	6	1738	20	1769	14
1677	14	1708	5	1739	17	1770	16
1678	15	1709	12	1740	25	1771	5
1679	9	1710	5	1741	1	1772	6
1680	17	1711	0	1742	31	1773	6
1681	38	1712	8	1743	10	1774	2
1682	25	1713	6	1744	35	1775	1
1683	12	1714	20	1745	41	1776	1
1684	7	1715	23	1746	32	1777	1
1685	8	1716	0	1747	37	1778	0
1686	3	1717	0	1748	33	1779	0
1687	5	1718	2	1749	31	1780	3
1688	0	1719	0	1750	25	1781	9
1689	5	1720	10	1751	34	1782	5
1690	1	1721	4	1752	31	1783	15
1691	1	1722	11	1753	27	1784	9
1692	13	1723	5	1754	11	1785	13
1693	10	1724	3	1755	10	1786	10
1694	6	1725	0	1756	1	1787	9
1695	9	1726	0	1757	7	1788	8
1696	5	1727	41	1758	6	1789	5
1697	14	1728	31	1759	3	1790	12
1698	0	1729	25	1760	0	1791	4
1699	8	1730	26	1761	0	1792	4
1700	13	1731	13	1762	10	1793	5
1701	3	1732	5	1763	5	1794	11
1702	2	1733	32	1764	2	1795	8
1703	1	1734	13	1765	13	1796	3
1704	10	1735	10	1766	14		

VII. BASEL. CASES OF PROFANITY BEFORE THE REFORMATION CHAMBER

FIFTEEN DATES SELECTED FROM 111 YEARS

Date	Total Cases	Profanity
1681	289	10
1682	156	5
1692	99	0
1705	102	1
1715	90	0
1720	80	0
1727	283	2
1733	209	0
1737	152	2
1745	82	0
1751	40	0
1755	16	0
1766	67	0
1770	62	0
1794	126	0

(108 Dancing)

VIII. BASEL. REFORMATIONS-KAMMER. SELECTED YEARS

Date	Dress Women	Dress Men	Sunday outside	Sunday Misc.	Dancing	Total Cases	Dismissed
1681	134	7	84	9	30	287	76
1682	45	3	66	31	6	156	
1692	16	6	25	12	40	99	
1700	13	1	7	6	33	60	
1705	44	0	49	3	1	102	
1709	62	0	39	14	1	118	
1715	8	0	54	14	10	90	56
1718	0	0	0	0	10	10	10
1720	0	0	80				32
1727	210	9	41	3	0	283	93
1733	98	5	30	19	45	209	106
1737	51	8	25	2	39	152	122
1745	30	9	8	26		82	37
1751	2	0	6	13	10	40	6
1755	6	0	7	1	2	16	11
1762	12	2	0	0	3	23	10
1766	31	0		4	9	67	27
1770	34	12	7	0	2	62	23
1794	3	0	6	0	108	126	2

IX. WEDDINGS. BASEL AND ZURICH

BASEL. CASES BEFORE THE REFORMATION CHAMBER

YEARS SELECTED BECAUSE OF LARGE NUMBER OF PROSECUTIONS OF VARIOUS KINDS.

1687. Sept. 28. Dancing. Host fined 50 sh. 12 musicians 10 sh. each.
Dancing. 7 or more persons. Landlord fined.
Oct. 5. Dancing. Host fined 50 sh. Another wedding, delinquents not given.
1714. Steward of Smith Gild allowed dancing. Fine 25 sh. Musicians 10 sh.
1727. Excess guests 3.
1737. Excess hours 1.
1741. A few weddings handled. Only one meeting that year.
1750. Excess guests. Excuse some honorary.
1751. An Afterwedding. Excuse not the same guests.
1751. Wedding excess hours 4. Complaint weddings held in private houses. No lists.
1752. Steward of Saffron Gild. Excess guests. Finally fined for 2 extra.
1765. Guests 55 instead of 50. Host fined 20 pounds.
1766. Poultry at wedding dinner. Dismissed with warning.
1770. Holding back list of guests. Fined 20 pounds.
1795. Wedding dance and Afterwedding. Several persons.
1795. Great wedding in Löwen Gild. 21 guests arraigned.

WEDDINGS. ZURICH. CASES BEFORE THE REFORMATION CHAMBER.

1711. Shooting, dancing, excess dress of bride.
1712-13. Dress only.
1714. Excess feasting, foreign poultry 1, dancing, dress.
1716. Shooting.
1717. Several large weddings fined. Excess horse parade.
1718. Shooting 3. Colored ribbons several.
1721. Men's dress.
1722. Unlawful jewelry.
1727. Excess in clothing 2 or 3.
1728-1739. Shooting 4 cases.
1741. Gold decorated carriage.
1742-1761. Shooting cases 4.
1765. Sending gift of dower-chest. Eight ladies warned.
1766. Wedding feast excess 1.
1775. Guest not a relative 1.
1779. Shooting 2.
1784. Horse parade at wedding. 11 persons in one case.

X. ZURICH. SESSIONS OF REFORMATION CHAMBER.

CASES OF COSTUME EIGHTEENTH CENTURY

Date	Sessions	Dress Women	Dress Men	Date	Sessions	Dress Women	Dress Men
1709	10	17	2	1755	20	34	1
1710	44	247	70	1756	10	1	0
1711	41	50	16	1757	14	0	0
1712	20	6	7	1758	13	2	0
1713	25	49	1	1759	13	0	0
1714	39	18	3	1760	11	0	0
1715	30	43	7	1761	7	0	0
1716	35	38	5	1762	15	0	3
1717	27	1	0	1763	7	0	0
1718	30	6	14	1764	30	27	22
1719	30	8	52	1765	27	10	16
1720	29	0	1	1766	16	0	3
1721	21	0	4	1767	24	0	1
1722	19	24	1	1768	10	0	0
1723	25	18	1	1769	20	0	0
1724	35	87	12	1770	19	3	0
1725	27	10		1771	11	0	0
1726	20	0	1	1772	12	0	0
1727	28	6	0	1773	5	0	1
1728	29	58	0	1774	11	0	0
1729	26	18	3	1775	14	0	1
1730-1733	No record			1776	14	7	2
1734	20	8	0	1777	13	6	1
1735	28	25	1	1778	29	4	27
1736	32	13	5	1779	27	7	10
1737	26	46	6	1780	17	14	0
1738	31	0	1	1781	16	4	2
1739	30	9	1	1782	14	0	2
1740	25	15	0	1783	14	0	0
1741	32	4	1	1784	10	3	0
1742	22	26	0	1785	17	2	2
1743	23	7	0	1786	13	0	1
1744	22	9	0	1787	14	11	1
1745	17	11	0	1788	18	2	0
1746	11	0	0	1789	17	0	0
1747	5	1	1	1790	11	0	0
1748	17	1	2	1791	14	1	0
1749	16	0	0	1792	9	0	0
1750	12	0	0	1793	12	0	0
1751	9	4	0	1794	16	0	0
1752	20	7	0	1795	11	0	0
1753	15	0	0	1796	9	0	0
1754	11	0	0	1797	6	0	0

XI. UNLAWFUL DRESS

Comparison of Prosecutions, Bern and Basel, Seventeenth Century

	BERN.				BASEL.		
Date	Sessions	Dress Women	Dress Men	Date	Sessions	Dress Women	Dress Men
1676	18	80	16	1674	4	5	0
1681	7	17		1681	38	134	7
1682	12	94	25	1682	25	48	3
1692	19	163	67	1692	13	16	6
1693	43	219	93				

Comparison of Prosecutions, Basel and Zurich, Eighteenth Century

	BASEL.				ZURICH.		
Date	Sessions	Dress Women	Dress Men	Date	Sessions	Dress Women	Dress Men
1709	12	62	0	1709	10	17	2
1715	23	8	0	1715	44	43	7
1720	10	0	0	1720	29	0	
1727	41	210	9	1727	28	6	0
1733	32	98	5	1733	Record missing		
1737	31	51	8	1737	26	46	6
1745	41	30	9	1745	17	11	0
1751	34	2	0	1751	12	4	0
1755	10	6	0	1755	20	34	1
1762	10	12	2	1762	15	0	3
1766	14	31	0	1766	16	0	3
1770	16	34	12	1770	19	3	0
1794	11	3	0	1794	16	0	0

SELECTED BIBLIOGRAPHY

ORDINANCES

The acts of the City Councils of Basel, Bern and Zurich have been carefully preserved in manuscript and print. The sumptuary ordinances alone make a formidable list for each town. Let it suffice to say that these laws were revised and reënacted at frequent intervals and after 1498 began to appear in print in pamphlet form in order that they might be read from the pulpits. Of these prints the author possesses numerous copies and has consulted many more.

The earlier ordinances of Bern have been printed in the collection of Welti and the summary of Haller, those of Zurich by Zeller-Werdmüller. The full titles are given below.

Welti, F. E. *Die Rechtsquellen des Kantons Bern. Band I. Das Stadtrecht von Bern, 1218-1539.* Arau, 1902.

Zeller-Werdmüller, H. *Die Zürcher Stadtbücher des XIV und XV Jahrhunderts.* 3 Bde. 1899-1906.

Haller, B. *Bern in seinen Rathsmanuelen.* 3 vols. Bern, 1900-1902.
   Acts of the City Council of Bern summarized. Ordinances regulating clothing vol. 2, p. 365.

Zurich. *Sammlung der bürgerlichen und polizei Gesetze und Ordnungen Löblicher Stadt und Landschaft Zürich.* 6 vols. 1793.
   Laws of the second half of the 18th century.

MANUSCRIPTS

Basel. *Reformations Straffbuch. 1674-1796.* Contains the minutes of the Reformations-Kammer continuous during 122 years. Ms. Staats-Archiv, Basel Stadt.

Bern. The early records of the execution of the sumptuary laws would naturally be found in the minutes of the *Chor-gericht* (Consistorium) up to the formation of special commissions and finally the Reformations-Kammer. From 1676 to 1696 except for a short break the cases of this latter court are recorded in an *Executions Manual,* the manuscript of which is kept in the Stadt Bibliothek of Bern. For nearly a century following only fragments of this record have survived. From 1781 to 1797 a *Manual des Reformations Raths* gives the minutes of the last few years of its existence. Ms. in the Staats-Archiv of Bern. See also Studer, F. below.

Zurich. Under a commission called " *die Verordneten zur Uebersicht des Grossen Mandats* " and later under a *Reformations-Kammer* the execution of the sumptuary ordinances in the seventeenth century is sufficiently established but the record of that period is badly broken. The problems of the court are often seen in the cases and questions submitted to the city council. For the eighteenth century the evidence is excellent. For the ninety years between 1709 and 1799 the minutes are complete except for the years 1730 to 1733.

Zurich. *Protokoll der Reformations Kammer. 1709 to 1729, 1734 to 1799.* Ms. Stadt Archiv Zürich.

PRINTED

Brief references to books through which the perspective of Swiss history may be enlarged in connection with the special topics treated in this volume.

Heinemann, Franz. *Weltliche Gebräuche und Sitten.* Part of *Bibliographie der Schweizerischen Landeskunde. Heft IV der Kulturgeschichte und Volkskunde (Folklore) der Schweiz.* Fascikel V 5. 2 vols. Bern, 1910-13.
Consult index under *Hochzeit, Luxus, Trachten, Kleider, Tanzen, Sonntags Heiligung,* etc.

Studer, F. *Verhandlungen der Reformations Kammer von 1676 bis 1696.* Berner Taschenbuch, 1879, p. 207 etc.

Wackernagel, Rudolf. *Geschichte der Stadt Basel.* 3 vols. in 4. Basel, 1907-1927.
History of Basel from its beginnings to the adoption of the Reformation.

Heusler, Andreas. *Geschichte der Stadt Basel.* 3rd Ed. Basel, 1918.
Short popular account from the beginning to 1848.

Geering, Tr. *Handel und Industrie der Stadt Basel.* Basel, 1886.

Dändliker, Karl. *Geschichte der Stadt und des Kantons Zurich.* 3 vols. Zürich, 1908-12.
A narrative from the beginning to 1892.

Franklin, Alfred. *Les Magasins de Nouveautés.* (Series *La Vie Privée d'Autrefois.*) Paris, 1894.

Greenfield, Kent Roberts. *Sumptuary Law in Nürnberg: a study in paternal government.* The Johns Hopkins University Studies in Historical and Political Science, Series 36, No. 2. Baltimore 1918.
The period covered extends from the fourteenth to the end of the fifteenth century.

Baldwin, F. Elizabeth. *Sumptuary Legislation and Personal Regulation in England.* The Johns Hopkins University Studies in Historical and Political Science, Series 45, No. 1. Baltimore, 1926.
Treats the subject from the reign of Edward III to that of James I when regulations of dress practically came to an end.

ILLUSTRATIONS

Contemporary pictures of persons and costumes can be readily found in the histories of art and when these are attributed to distinguished artists the author's name is noted below his work. For others equally valuable for the purposes of this book the author wishes to express his obligation to the authors and compilers whose works are named below.

Chronik der Burg Wildegg von 1584 bis 1684. Eight pictures.

E. von Rodt, *Bern im Sechzehnten Jahrhundert.* The Chorgericht.

D. Burckhardt-Wertheman, *Häuser und Gestalten aus Basels Vergangenheit.* Six pictures.

Otto Henne am Rhyn, *Kulturgeschichte des Deutschen Volkes,* Band 2. From two complicated pictures of fashions numerous drawings have been selected and details completed by Dr. Emily Emmart.

Johannes Sutz, *Schweizer Geschichte für das Volk erzählt.* Five groups.

Alfred Franklin, *Les Magasins de Nouveautés.* Group and figure.

Karl Dändliker, *Geschichte der Schweiz.* Four drawings of costume.

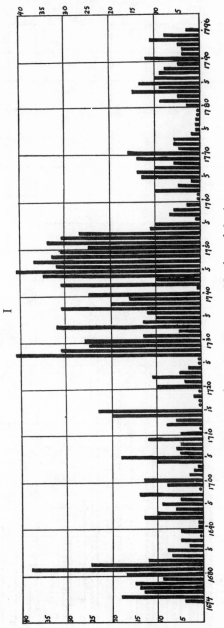

Basel. Reformations-Kammer. Number of Sessions.

II

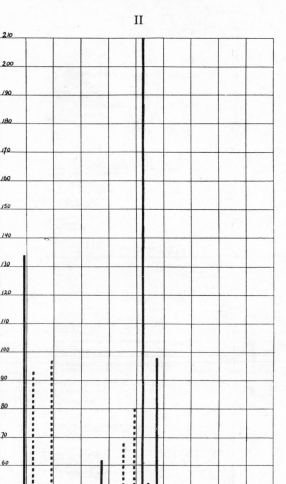

Basel. Dress and Sabbath Observance.

III

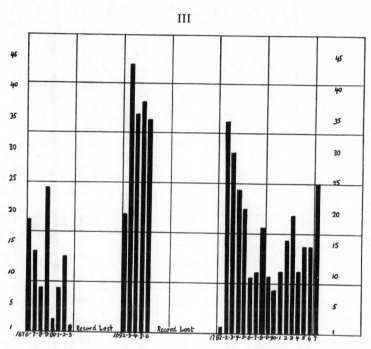

Bern. Sessions of Reformations-Rath.

IV

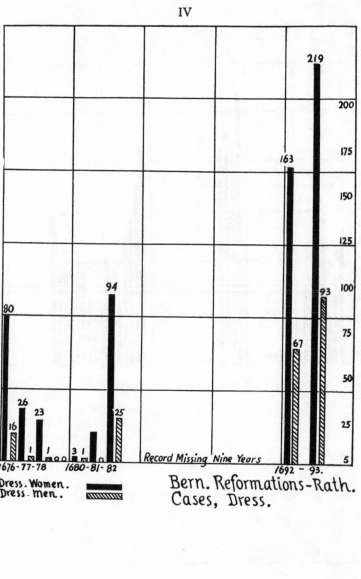

Record Missing Nine Years

Dress. Women.
Dress. men.

Bern. Reformations-Rath.
Cases, Dress.

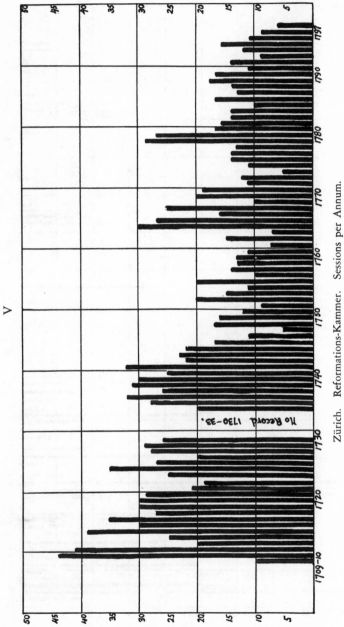

V

Zürich. Reformations-Kammer. Sessions per Annum.

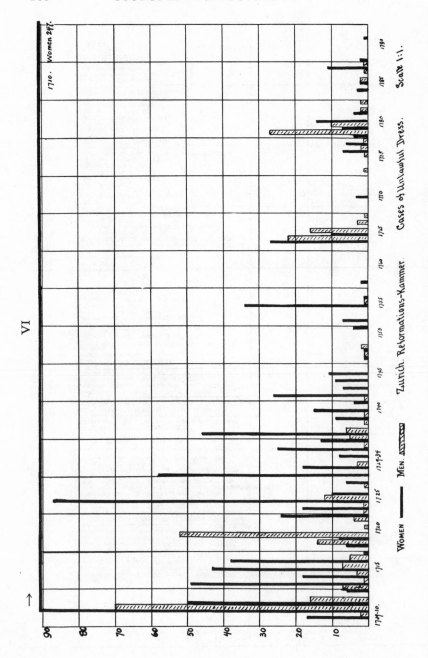

VI

Zürich. Reformations-Kammer. Cases of Unlawful Dress. Scale 1:1.

Women ▬▬▬ Men ▨▨▨

INDEX

169